Social Media
for Lawyers
THE NEXT FRONTIER

Carolyn Elefant and Nicole Black

ABA Law Practice Management Section
MARKETING • MANAGEMENT • TECHNOLOGY • FINANCE

Commitment to Quality: The Law Practice Management Section is committed to quality in our publications. Our authors are experienced practitioners in their fields. Prior to publication, the contents of all our books are rigorously reviewed by experts to ensure the highest quality product and presentation. Because we are committed to serving our readers' needs, we welcome your feedback on how we can improve future editions of this book.

Cover design by RIPE Creative.

Printed in the United States of America.

12 11   5 4

Library of Congress Cataloging-in-Publication Data

Elefant, Carolyn.
    Social media for lawyers: the next frontier / by Carolyn Elefant and Nicole Black.
        p. cm.
    Includes index.
    ISBN 978-1-60442-920-6
    1. Internet in legal services—United States. 2. Law offices—United States—Computer network resources. 3. Online social networks—United States. I. Black, Nicole, 1970– II. Title.
    KF320.A9E44 2010
    347.00285′4678—dc22

                                                      2010012953

Discounts are available for books ordered in bulk. Special consideration is given to state bars, CLE programs, and other bar-related organizations. Inquire at Book Publishing, American Bar Association, 321 N. Clark Street, Chicago, Illinois 60654.

Contents

About the Authors

Carolyn Elefant is a practicing attorney with her own firm, the Law Offices of Carolyn Elefant, in Washington, D.C. Carolyn is creator of MyShingle.com, the longest running (since 2002) blog and resource for solo and small practitioners. She is also author of *Solo by Choice: How to Be the Lawyer You Always Wanted to Be* (Decision Books, 2008). From March 2006 through September 2009, Carolyn coauthored Incisive Media/Law.com's popular Legal Blog Watch blog. She also speaks before bar associations, law schools and law firms about twenty-first century solo and small firm practice, the future of the legal profession, and the ethics of social media. Carolyn resides in the Washington, D.C., area with her husband and two daughters.

Nicole Black is of counsel to Fiandach and Fiandach and is also the founder of lawtechTalk.com, a company that educates lawyers regarding technology issues and provides legal technology consulting services. She coauthors *Criminal Law in New York*, a West-Thomson treatise and is currently working on a book about cloud computing for lawyers that will be published by the American Bar Association in late 2010.

Nicole also publishes four legal blogs, including "Practicing Law in the 21st Century" (**http://21stcenturylaw.wordpress.com/**), writes a weekly column for the Daily Record focusing on a variety of topics, including law and technology issues, and regularly speaks at conferences regarding the intersection of law, technology and social media. She resides in Rochester, New York, with her husband and two children.

Acknowledgments

Carolyn Elefant

This book would not have come into being without the support and hard work of many others. Thanks to fellow ABA author Carole Levitt for recognizing the value of a book on social media for lawyers, shepherding the book through the initial approval stages and providing feedback on the first draft. Likewise, thanks to Tim Johnson for his editorial review as well as his tireless work to get the book to press in a timely manner.

As the prologue to the book notes, my coauthor Nicole Black and I have known each other five years, but until this project, we'd never had a chance to work together. There are few lawyers who are as savvy and intuitive about the future of law technology as Niki or who can write and speak about it with so much passion. Collaborating with Niki was a privilege.

Finally, I'm grateful to my techno-geek husband, Bruce, who nurtured my initial interest in technology by introducing me to email and the World Wide Web, and to my daughters, Elana and Mira, who through their (constant!) social media and technology give me a sneak-peek into what the future of law will look like.

Nicole Black

I would like to thank, first and foremost, my husband, Scott, and my children for their loving support and patience as I wrote this book. They are the reason for everything I do and without them I would be half the person that I am today.

I'm also very grateful to my brother, Jon, and my sister-in-law, Ellyn, for lending me their quiet home to use as my "office" when they were out of town. I'd never have been able to finish the bulk of my writing but for their generosity.

Thank you to all the legal professionals who took the time out of their busy schedules to answer our questions about their social media use and experiences. Their contributions added greatly to this book and are much appreciated.

I am also very grateful to my coauthor, Carolyn Elefant, for inviting me to write this book with her and for all of her advice and support over the years. I've learned so much from her and continue to do so every day.

Finally, I gratefully acknowledge the thoughtful guidance of our editor, Tim Johnson, and the rest of the ABA Law Practice Management Section publishing staff. They helped us make this book the best it could be.

low Pages to find a lawyer, or corporate counsel cracks open a tome of Martindale-Hubbell to locate representation in another jurisdiction. Instead, empowered by the deep pool of resources available online, consumers and corporate counsel alike are inclined to educate themselves about various legal issues through blogs, online video, and conversations in online community sites before they even compile a list of potential lawyers. Moreover, once prospective clients start to gather names of lawyers—either directly through Internet searches or via personal referrals—they then return back online to check out the lawyers' credentials, experience, and testimonials and get feedback from other clients and colleagues.

Further, recent studies show that consumers trust the information they locate online. The Pew Report (**http://hbr.harvardbusiness.org/ 2009/11/community-relations-20/ar/1**) found that nearly 40 percent of Americans doubted a medical professional's opinion or diagnosis because it conflicted with information they had found online. Likewise, consumers take peer reviews seriously, with 78 percent relying on ratings and reviews in making purchase decisions (**http://itpro marketer.com/2009/11/social-media-revolution/**).

Social media gives lawyers the tools to provide potential clients with the kind of in-depth information that they've come to expect online prior to making any kind of decision requiring a significant commitment of resources. Bottom line: If you're not using social media, you can't deliver the kind of information that today's clients demand before hiring a lawyer.

The Need for Personal Connections. Even as we spend more time online, as humans we still crave some form of personal connection. In business, personal connections continue to matter since we're more likely to do business with people whose company we enjoy.

Social media satisfies our longing for human contact and provides a tool for building trusted, multidimensional relationships. Platforms like Twitter and Facebook give lawyers a chance to reveal a little piece of personality or share tidbits about family, hobbies, and quirky likes and dislikes. Meanwhile, for those uncomfortable mixing business with pleasure, there are other tools—like blogging—for expressing your views and engaging in conversation about court cases or other legal matters. Whether it's through a recipe exchange or rooting for your favorite sports team on Twitter, or a heated discussion through blogging, the interactive nature of social media helps lawyers build deeper and more meaningful connections online, which eventually translates into offline business and friendship.

Social Media Is Fast and Cheap. In a society that's on the go 24-7, social media delivers the news at a record pace. A few minutes a day on Twitter can update participants on the news more quickly than scanning the newspaper. And as society continues to move at a record pace, social media's currency will become even more valuable. What's more, social media is largely free, which makes it harder to ignore.

2. A social media presence is a tool for achieving your goals and not, in itself, a goal.

You may be familiar with some of social media's power users owing to the media coverage that they've garnered—like David Barrett, who describes himself as "the most LinkedIn lawyer in the world" with over 12,000 connections on LinkedIn; solo lawyer Richard Vetsein, who gathered 600 fans for his law firm's Facebook Fan Page in a matter of weeks; or Rex Gradeless, a recent law graduate who has over 73,000 followers on Twitter.

While these numbers are impressive, don't let them intimidate you or prevent you from jumping on board with social media. We can't emphasize enough that social media is a tool which can be used to achieve your professional goals, not a goal in and of itself. In contrast to a frequent flier program where accumulated miles translate into a free trip, racking up friends, followers, or blog visitors just for the sake of doing so won't necessarily confer rewards like more referrals or clients. Moreover, you're likely to annoy your colleagues and waste your time with obsessive efforts to gain more followers.

Actually, social media eliminates the need to generate a presence through big numbers, which is a loser's game, particularly for solo and small firm lawyers. Instead, social media gives you the ability to focus your message on your specific target audiences and develop a strategy tailored to carry out your goals.

3. Use of social media doesn't transform otherwise appropriate conduct into something unethical.

Many lawyers are hesitant to adopt social media, concerned that unresolved ethics issues could put them at risk of a grievance. What's important to understand, however, is that social media changes the medium,

not the message. In other words, lawyers don't check their ethics obliga-
tions at the social media portal. Even in this new frontier, the same familiar ethics rules guide lawyers' conduct.

For example, a communication that's inherently unethical—such as
revealing a client confidence—doesn't become any more acceptable when
the information is disclosed in a 140-character tweet [e.g., "In NYC court.
Client just told me that the heroin belonged to him! Ugh, case ruined."]
Conversely, a blog post analyzing a recent case or explaining how to file
for bankruptcy isn't transformed into bar-regulated advertising merely
because it's self-published online, whereas it would be viewed as harmless
if published in a law journal or as a newspaper column.

Once lawyers recognize that communications on social media don't differ
much from those in other arenas, they can readily conform their use of
social media tools to existing ethics requirements, just as they do for
other areas of their practice.

How This Book Is Organized

This book is organized as follows. Part I opens with a brief historic
overview of social media. We'll describe some of the current trends in
social media and share statistics on existing use. Thereafter, we'll show
why social media is important for lawyers and bust some of the myths
that deter lawyers from engaging social media. If you're new to social
media or are simply interested in reading a generalized overview of social
media, start with this section.

In Part II, we'll get down to brass bytes, with descriptions and screenshots
of various social media platforms, and guidance on how to seamlessly
coordinate, integrate, and promote your social media presence.

In Part III, we'll then focus on how to use social media to accomplish specific goals such as establishing expertise, building relationships with colleagues and engaging in damage control. In this section, we've adopted a
practical, goal-centric approach to implementing social media.

In Part IV, we'll focus on the nuts and bolts of setting up social media profiles and engaging in social media. We'll also discuss the dos and don'ts of
social media, including best practices and appropriate "net-iquette."

Finally, in Part V, we'll focus on the ethical and legal issues of social
media, including bar rules, Federal Trade Commission (FTC) disclosure
requirements, as well as copyright issues, defamation, damage control,
and in-house blogging policies. Then we'll conclude with our predictions
of where social media is headed in the future.

One topic we won't cover: For at least a decade, lawyers have been using the Internet, and more recently, social media as investigatory tools in legal matters. Because this book focuses on how lawyers can use social media to accomplish professional goals, such as networking with colleagues or establishing themselves as experts, social media as a discovery tool is beyond the scope of this book. If you're interested in that topic, consult *The Cybersleuth's Guide to the Internet* by Carole Levitt, JD, MLS and Mark E. Rosch.

PART ONE

Overview of
Social Media and
Its Role in the
Legal Profession

CHAPTER ONE

An Introduction to Social Media

A powerful global conversation has begun. Through the Internet, people are discovering and inventing new ways to share relevant knowledge with blinding speed.
> —*The Cluetrain Manifesto: End of Business as Usual* (2001)

Officially, social media is an umbrella term that encompasses the various activities that integrate technology and social interaction. It's also a fancy way to describe the zillions of conversations that people are having online 24/7.
> —Marta Kagan, *What . . . is Social Media: One Year Later* (2009)
> (online at slideshare.net)

What Is Social Media?

A little bit of history. . . . Once upon a time in the mid-1990s, the Internet was flat. Early versions of websites functioned as little more than glorified online versions of flat (hard copy) brochures, characterized by static content and limited substantive resources. Most pages were primitively designed, laden with blinking text or cockeyed tables and hard-to-remember URLs like **smithsmithandjoneslawfirm8757975.aol.com/html**. Sites grew stale, since updating content through file transfer protocol was a cumbersome task. And while site visitors could seek more information about a website via email and a website could link to other pages, Web 1.0 offered few opportunities for interaction or information sharing.

Enter Web 2.0, a catch phrase used to describe technology that "facilitates interactive information sharing, user-centered design and collaboration among users." [Source: **http://en.wikipeida.org/wiki/Web2.0**.] (As an aside, it bears noting that Wikipedia, a widely used, collaboratively authored online encyclopedia is one of Web 2.0's greatest success stories!) Web 2.0 technology spawned the birth of today's social media platforms, which include blogs, online directories with opportunities for client reviews and feedback, online community sites, and wikis.

Characteristics of Social Media
Social media applications share several common characteristics that make them particularly appealing.

High degree of user-friendliness
Virtually all social media platforms rely on highly user-friendly interfaces and require minimal technical skills to implement. In many cases, a lawyer can register for a social media site, create a profile, and begin using it in under an hour.

Customization
Customizability is at the heart of Web 2.0, and most social media tools let lawyers adapt their reach and scope to fit their needs. Lawyers can customize the look of social media sites by uploading logos and photographs and even changing the color or format. Lawyers can choose whom they want to friend, follow, or link to, which lawyers and colleagues they want to ask for testimonials, and whether or not to allow comments at blogs.

Privacy settings
Most social media tools include public and private settings, thereby letting lawyers control who can view content posted (or even who can search for them). Though the most stringent privacy settings won't prevent someone to whom you've granted access from taking a screenshot of a wall post or photo and redistributing it, copyright law may provide some protection against unauthorized redistribution.

User-generated content
Most of social media's content is generated by users. Users can self-publish articles on blogs or post them on other community sites, and they can comment or rate products. The ability of users to generate content, without any editing, oversight or selection process scares lawyers (who

may fear that clients or competitors will criticize them), but it also opens up opportunities for lawyers to disseminate their own information.

Free or low cost

One of the best features of today's social media applications is that they're free or low cost. Though some services offer premium add-ons, the free products are completely functional (the sole exception being free blog hosting platforms like blogger.com or wordpress.com, where we advise that you purchase a domain name and forward it[1] rather than settle for a URL like **www.iowalawyer.blogger.com**). In fact, these days, it's entirely possible (though not necessarily desirable) to maintain an online presence using only social media tools like LinkedIn, Avvo, and Twitter and not even spend the time or resources to create a website.

Professional-looking product

Today's social media tools generate a highly professional-looking product that you won't be ashamed to present to clients. The profiles provided at sites like LinkedIn or Avvo are light-years more elegant and functional than the clunky, poorly designed websites of yore.

Broad reach

Sites like Avvo or LinkedIn attract substantial traffic, so lawyers who list their profiles on these sites can boost their visibility and expand their online reach.

Open access platforms supporting integration and convergence

Increasingly, social media tools are converging with each other, adding tools and features that allow for integration of other platforms. For example, you may have noticed most blog posts include a widget that allows readers to send a post to another social media platform like Digg, Facebook, or Twitter. Likewise, Facebook and LinkedIn users can automatically display posts from their blogs or recent Tweets onto their Facebook and LinkedIn profile page. As social media matures, we predict that we'll see increased integration, thus enabling users to maintain a consistent online presence across all of the platforms upon which they participate.

---

[1] When you register a domain name, you can set it up to "point" at another site.

The Numbers

Without a doubt, social media sites are growing fast and furiously. Consider the traffic that these sites generate.[2]

Site	Number of Users	Monthly Traffic (December 2009)	Predominant Demographic
Facebook	350 million (site states)	117 Million	Ages: 35+ 33% $60k+ 58% 45% M, 55% F
MySpace	260 million (estimate, Gartner 2010 IT Reports)	55 Million	Ages: 18-34 58% $30-$60k 44% 51% M, 49% F
Twitter	18 million (Source: http://mashable.com/2009/09/14/twitter-2009-stats/)	23.6 Million	Ages: 35+ 42% $60k+ 52% 47% M, 53% F
LinkedIn	50+ million (Source: http://mashable.com/2009/10/14/linkedin-50-millon/)	30.7 Million	Ages: 35+ 77% $60k+ 69% 54% M, 46% F
Avvo	No data	240,000	Ages: 35-49 38% 43% M, 57% F [no info. Re: income]

As the statistics bear out, contrary to popular perception, users 35 and older, rather than teens and 20 somethings, dominate the top social media sites. Because most lawyers consider the 35+ demographic the sweet spot for marketing purposes, social media provides a powerful marketing tool.

Social media hasn't displaced blogging, however. According to Technorati's *State of the Blogosphere* Report, blogging activity doubles in size every 200 days, with 175,000 new blogs created every day over the past three years. Of course, it's necessary to keep these statistics in perspective, because 45 percent of bloggers stop blogging after just three months.

FACTOID #1

Years to Reach 50 Million Users: Radio (38 Years), TV (13 Years), Internet (4 Years), iPod (3 Years) . . . Facebook added 100 million users in less than 9 months . . . iPhone applications hit 1 billion in 9 months.[3]

---

[2] Information in the above table on user numbers is derived from Mashable.com and site stats. Traffic statistics and demographic information contained in the table were derived from quantcast.com, or found at the individual sites.

[3] http://socialnomics.net/2009/08/11/statistics-show-social-media-is-bigger-than-you-think/

Still, many adults don't yet read blogs. According to Pew Internet and American Life Report (2009), 54 percent of college students read blogs, compared to just 36 percent of adults. But 21 percent of Fortune 1000 senior executives read business-related blogs at least once a week or more frequently, which means that blogs can be effective in helping lawyers reach this target audience.

Where Is Social Media Headed?

So how big can social media get? We believe that social media is still in its infancy and will continue to grow steadily at least for the next five years. Lawyers who come on board now will have an advantage as social media gains momentum in years to come.

CHAPTER TWO

Why Social Media Is Gaining Traction with Lawyers

WE'VE MENTIONED SOME OF the more general reasons—usability, low cost, and interactivity—that have contributed to the growing adoption of social media by society at large. But there are additional reasons, unique to the legal industry, that explain why social media is starting to establish a toehold in our typically conservative and otherwise decade-behind-the-times profession.

1. Lawyers have long recognized the value of networking, and social media enhances their ability to do so effectively.

All lawyers understand the importance of networking. Interacting with colleagues, current clients, and potential clients is a surefire way to increase business opportunities and referrals. In the past, networking traditionally occurred in many forums, including events sponsored by bar associations or other professional organizations, on the golf course, or while participating in community activities. Not all lawyers relished the concept of networking, but the general school of thought was that it was a necessary part of doing business, and staying cooped-up in an office day in and day out was counterproductive to rainmaking.

With the recent explosion of social media and online networking opportunities, however, traditional notions regarding networking may no

Is Social Media Different for Lawyers?

(The following is an edited excerpt of a conversation on Twitter regarding the effective use of social media to promote legal services.)

♦ <u>nikiblack</u>: Social media for lawyers is a different focus than for most businesses. For lawyers it's about creating effective online presence, networking & establishing expertise.

♦ <u>SCartierLiebel</u>: Social media is about people, so not passionate about law firms . . . but can be very engaged with their lawyer . . .

♦ <u>JohnFMoore</u>: (It's about creating effective online presence, networking & establishing expertise) | All biz should use this way, right?

♦ <u>nikiblack</u>: I agree. But other businesses can create viral campaigns, create a tribe of followers that evangelize their product. Not the law . . .

♦ <u>nikiblack</u>: Social media goals are different for lawyers. With specific goals in mind, you then choose appropriate social media platforms & levels of participation.

♦ <u>jeffrey_brandt</u>: Different than what? A widget/product company? Yes, but other service industries use social media—how are lawyers different?

♦ <u>mikemac29</u>: Law isn't a service industry people rush to interact with, or feel passionate about, it's more like a utility co.

♦ <u>nikiblack</u>: Exactly—I totally agree. People reluctantly use/pay for lawyers. Hard to create a passionate following when starting w/that!

♦ <u>nikiblack</u>: Lawyers' services aren't "sexy"—there's no hook. Can't create sweepstakes/contest for reduced services to increase interest.

♦ <u>SCartierLiebel</u>: It's what you do with the platforms to push out compelling info about lawyers to create evangelists and interest. It's called PR.

♦ <u>SCartierLiebel</u>: They may just evangelize you differently based upon non-legal interests. This may be the key.

CHAPTER THREE

Busting the Legal Profession's Ten Myths of Social Media

IN THE PREVIOUS CHAPTER, we described the increasing importance of social media in the legal profession. Even so, we recognize that many lawyers' misconceptions about social media are deeply entrenched and must be addressed head on. So here, we'll bust the ten most common myths about social media.

1. There's no point in using social media in my practice because none of my target clients use it.

Even if your target client population isn't online, that's no reason to dismiss social media. For starters, you can use social media to cultivate client referrals rather than directly generate client leads. For example, by blogging about a particular issue intelligently, you may impress other lawyers with your analysis, which in turn can lead to referrals for cases that they can't handle.

> **FACTOID #2**
>
> Social media has overtaken porn as the #1 activity on the Web.[1]

---

[1] http://socialnomics.net/2009/08/11/statistics-show-social-media-is-bigger-than-you-think/

Moreover, direct client generation isn't the only reason to engage in social media. You can also use social media tools like Twitter to track emerging issues in an area or launch a blog to establish expertise in a particular subject matter which can lead to speaking engagements or media appearances, and in turn may generate clients and referrals.

Further, even if your clients aren't using social media now, expect that to change in the next three to five years as the first wave of college students raised on social media enters the workplace and becomes potential consumers of legal services. As we've already mentioned, users who are age 35 and up represent the fastest growing social media demographic. So by engaging social media now, you gain a first mover advantage.

2. Social media is undignified for lawyers.

This same criticism could be leveled against any type of lawyer communication, from a newspaper advertisement to in-person "meet and greets" at a party. No doubt, you've seen your share of cheesy newspaper ads or billboards by lawyers, or attended a conference where a loudmouth lawyer passed out business cards while glad-handing with participants like a used-car salesman.

Just as lawyers aren't forced to employ these types of techniques in traditional advertising, social media doesn't compel a race to the bottom. Social media doesn't require you to drown Twitter followers in a stream of tweets or write blog posts with screaming headlines like "14-year-old boy killed by drunk trucker!!" and to follow each post with a blazing yellow box urging readers to call you about a legal problem.

Sure, like any other marketing tool, social media can be abused, but at the same time, lawyers can use it for loftier purposes. Because of social media's low cost barriers and ease of use, lawyers can upload forms and e-books to sites like JD Supra, create short educational pod or video casts, or write a series of how-to articles at their blog to help potential clients better understand their rights and to educate the public on the legal process. In short, by engaging in these types of educational-based marketing that social media readily supports, lawyers can improve their public image. What's so undignified about that?

3. Social media is a waste of time—I don't want to learn about Joe's breakfast on Twitter or read about Jane's kids on Facebook.

Do you brush by the receptionist when she shares news of her learning-disabled son's most recent accomplishments? Do you avoid law firm get-togethers or bar association happy hours because people engage in idle chatter rather than talk shop? Even in a traditional offline work setting, it's not unusual for lawyers and their colleagues to engage in personal banter or discuss their family or hobbies.

There's a good reason why so many business deals are closed on the golf course or at the ballpark. Clients prefer to do business with lawyers with whom they share common interests and whose company they enjoy both in and outside the office. Like the water cooler or the ballpark, social media facilitates more casual interaction between lawyers and their colleagues and clients. In doing so, it enables the kind of trusted relationships and lasting friendships that enrich and add dimension to our otherwise stressful and confined professional lives.

4. My colleagues and clients will think that I have too much time on my hands if they see me blogging or tweeting all the time.

Image matters in the legal profession, so it's not unreasonable to consider how clients and colleagues will view the level of your participation in social media. Incessant tweeting or Facebooking can convey that you're less than busy or all too willing to disrupt work on client matters, neither of which will make a favorable impression. Plus, even if you're using a virtual assistant or auto-feed functions to generate tweets or posts (and therefore, not taking time out of your day), a constant barrage of status updates, announcements, and links annoys other users and ultimately leads them to unfollow.

So, set a schedule for social media—perhaps logging on for a block of time at the start and close of your day, with perhaps another segment in between. Write blog posts in batches and set them to auto-post throughout the week, leverage the skills of a virtual assistant or college or law student to update online profiles and upload documents to sites like JD

Supra. You might even write a blog post or a blurb for your website explaining how you manage social media so that clients will get a sense of your efficiency and ability to leverage technology to multitask.

5. I've heard stories of clients trying to friend their lawyers on Facebook, or worse, writing negative reviews of them at client rating sites. I'd rather avoid that kind of thing altogether.

As the saying goes, you can run from social media—but you can't hide. Much as you'd prefer to avoid using social media, you may find yourself dragged into the fray. After all, nothing prevents a disgruntled client from posting negative reviews at sites like Yelp [*see*, for example, **http://www.yelp.com/topic/new-york-review-lawyers**] or an envious competitor from swiping large chunks of your blog content and disseminating it, without attribution, on his website.

First of all, most lawyers' concerns about negative ratings are overblown. Think about it—isn't it more fun to share information about a terrific hole-in-the-wall restaurant that your friends wouldn't have discovered on their trip rather than harping on places they should steer clear of? As it turns out, that's how most consumers approach online ratings: the vast majority of product reviews left by consumers on websites are positive. [Bazaarvoice Study via Econsultancy.com Blog (December 2007).] The Bazaarvoice study found that 90 percent of consumers who comment on product sites do so to inform others' purchasing decisions, while 79 percent wrote reviews to reward the company by raving about its product. Thus, if you avoid ratings sites like Avvo for fear of criticism, most likely, you'll miss out on compliments instead.

In addition, even though there will always be a small handful of ne'er-do-wells who criticize lawyers or steal content, social media can help contain the damage. By employing social media tools like real-time Web search or RSS feeds, lawyers can monitor what's said about them online, discover damaging information immediately and try to nip it in the bud (perhaps through a polite take-down request) instead of having it crop up several months later during a Google search by a prospective client. Further, by familiarizing themselves with how social media works, lawyers can avoid inadvertently embarrassing themselves—such as by posting suggestive comments to a friend on a Facebook page that turns out to be accessible to clients (use the message function, not the public wall post!) or turning a minor mishap into a public relations nightmare by taking a heavy-handed approach (as in the Nixon Peabody case, discussed in Chapter 14).

Lawyers can also use social media proactively. As we'll discuss, lawyers can e-shame a lawyer who stole another's content or generate positive reviews from satisfied clients at sites like Avvo or LinkedIn. By taking proactive steps, you can overshadow the grousing of a single malcontent.

Bottom line: in today's interconnected world, there's no such thing as opting out of social media. Instead of fearing or ignoring the inevitable, lawyers should learn to use social media to control and manage their online reputation.

6. Social media is simply too time consuming for a busy lawyer like me.

If that's your attitude towards social media, you may not be busy for long. Increasingly, consumers are using the Internet for much more than buying books and gadgets online. For example, a full 45 percent of consumers turn to social media in times of trouble for assistance with real estate, health, or tech problems [Source: Pew Report, 2009]. Likewise, demand for consumer reviews of service providers continues to grow, as evidenced by the popularity of sites like Angie's List, which rates home contractors (and receives more than 1 million visits a year) and the proliferation of sites that rate doctors [**http://blogs.wsj.com/health/2009/07/22/new-online-doctor-rating-site-treads-carefully/**]. The legal profession won't remain immune from these trends for much longer and if you haven't invested the time to cultivate an online presence or brand, you're likely to be overlooked.

Never fear—there are plenty of ways that you can work social media into a busy schedule. In fact, social media is far more cost and time efficient than traditional marketing methods, such as speaking engagements (which require lengthy prep and possibly out-of-town travel), advertisements (cost prohibitive for many lawyers), or networking lunches (nothing takes a bite out of a day like a two-hour bar lunch). And, best of all, your online networking can be incorporated into a daily routine without sacrificing time with family (like evening networking functions or out-of-town trips).

Let's face it, most social networking activities—such as updating a profile, posting a status report on Facebook, drafting a quick blog post, or reading through an RSS feed—don't require the same level of focus as an appellate brief or complex transaction. Generally, you can accomplish them while watching TV with your partner or spouse, or alongside your kids as they do their homework. And with mobile applications available for many social media activities, you can engage while waiting in line to go through security at the courthouse or while waiting in the carpool pickup line. As we will discuss, there are a host of tips for efficiently managing social media, including delegating ministerial tasks, carving out blocks of time to avoid "social-media seep" and repurposing content.

7. I'm a gregarious person and prefer to meet others face-to-face. With social media, I'll be stuck behind a computer screen 24-7.

Social media won't force you to sacrifice face-to-face meetings. Recent studies show [Pew Report 2009] that participation in online social media actually facilitates and increases interaction offline. For starters, social media tools like Twitter, blogs, or Facebook help disseminate information about offline events, thus increasing attendance and providing face-time aficionados with an endless list of activities to attend. Moreover, many social networking tools like Meetup, or Twitter (with its Tweet-ups) actively encourage users to organize in-person meetings or get together offline.

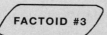

FACTOID #3

One out of eight couples married in the U.S. last year met via social media.[2]

In addition, social media can serve as an icebreaker, thus making in-person meetings more inviting for shy or less socially confidant lawyers. Social media gives you an opportunity to get to know colleagues online, so by the time you meet in person, approaching a colleague is far less awkward and the resulting conversations flow easily. So don't worry—in-person interaction isn't going the way of the dinosaur and we don't believe it ever will. Instead, social media will enhance the quality and enjoyment factor of face-to-face networking events and lead to richer, more satisfying offline connections rather than the other way around.

---

[2] **http://socialnomics.net/2009/08/11/statistics-show-social-media-is-bigger-than-you-think/**

8. If I give away free advice through blogging or responding to questions at directory sites, why would anyone hire me? Plus, what's to prevent competitors from stealing my content?

Remember the old maxim "Why buy the cow if you can get the milk for free"? In today's world, that adage no longer holds true. For starters, with an abundance of free resources and services online—like Wikipedia, Gmail, Google Voice, logo design, video games, and forms for simple wills or LLCs, consumers are no longer willing to pay for basic services or information. If your website doesn't offer a free e-book or guide on filing for bankruptcy or an extensive list of FAQs, clients will move along to the next site. In short, for lawyers seeking to do business online, free is no longer optional.

At the same time, far from deterring sales, free access to information whets consumers' appetite for fee-based services. As Chris Anderson explains in his book, *Free: The Future of a Radical Price*, even in a time of free, people will pay:

> People will pay to save time. People will pay to lower risk. People will pay for things they love. People will pay if you make them (once they're hooked).

In other words, by letting consumers or colleagues sample your work product—in the form of sample pleadings at JD Supra or a series of posts on how to file a patent—you'll make them realize, by showing rather than telling, why they need to hire you. As for the problem of competitors swiping material, you need to remain vigilant in monitoring use of your blog posts and vigorously enforcing your copyright. Fortunately, plagiarism can get a lawyer sanctioned by the bar, which, hopefully, serves as a sufficient deterrent to unauthorized use.

9. I've thought about getting onboard with social media, but it seems that it's already dominated by people with thousands of followers. It's going to take too much time to play catch-up.

Don't panic. Despite all the hype, we're still in the nascent stages of social media. Though some early lawyer-adapters with hundreds of connections on LinkedIn or thousands of followers on Twitter attract much attention, they're far from the norm.

More importantly, focusing on numbers misses the point of social media. Social media's advantage over traditional Internet marketing is that it allows for narrowly focused activities directed at your target market.

Back in the day of traditional websites, a lawyer with a general business practice would have been foolish to set up a site directed exclusively at home-based entrepreneurs living in Western Iowa because the costs of creating the site and optimizing its SEO could have been as high as $10,000 to $15,000, thus outweighing the benefits of any potential business. Instead, the lawyer would have set up a single site, with a page devoted to home-based entrepreneurs, and hoped for the best. But with social media, a lawyer can, with little effort, build a hub to attract this particular group of prospects by creating a blog (addressing legal issues for home-based entrepreneurs and perhaps profiling a few), sponsoring meetups, posting slides from the events on SlideShare, and following business owners in the community. Sure, the social media campaign might yield far less traffic than a grand website, but the quality of the leads is far better and more likely to convert to clients.

10. My teenager can teach me everything I need to know about social media.

Sure, your teenager can teach you a few things about the basics of social media, like how to create a Facebook account or set up a blog. If you're a complete novice, spend a couple of days observing how your children, grandchildren, or younger friends integrate social media applications into their day-to-day lives. In fact, observing his university-aged son's sophisticated use of Facebook (for managing contacts, organizing events, and keeping up with friends' activities) convinced Richard Susskind that "Facebook-like technology will become indispensable to lawyers in communicating with clients" [*The End of Lawyers: Rethinking the Future of the Legal Profession*].

Still, in order to really leverage the power of social media and build your online reputation and brand or generate business, you'll have to go beyond what a teenager can teach you. This book provides one resource, as do blogs like Mashable.com, and Socialmedialawstudent.com, which offer up-to-date information on trends in social media. You can also find free or inexpensive seminars on social media sponsored by companies like Avvo, G2Media, Lexblog, Martindale-Hubbell, the ABA, and state and local bar associations.

As for hiring a social media consultant, that's your call. But in our view, we'd advise against doing so until you first gain some practical social media experience on your own. Familiarity with what is feasible using social media will enable you to evaluate the consultant's proposed plan in an informed manner and, more importantly, ensure that it's ethically compliant. In the absence of vigorous oversight, "outsourcing marketing = outsourcing ethics," as *New York Personal Injury Attorney* blogger Eric Turkewitz has said. Additionally, it's important to realize that because the phenomenon of social media is so new, bonafide "experts" haven't yet emerged.

PART TWO

Tools of the Trade

Comparative Chart: Categories of Social Media

Category	Functions and Features	Examples	Convergence, Integration and Crossover
Directories and Profiles	Resume-type listing with ratings by colleagues and clients	Avvo, LinkedIn, Justia	Integrates blogs, Facebook, and Twitter feeds
Communication	Disseminates writings, thoughts, and information on ongoing basis or even realtime	Blogs, Twitter (micro-blog)	Widgets allow auto-posting to directory sites
Communities	Collegial or personal interaction at enclosed site, often less formal setting; support uploads of photos and other media	Facebook, LinkedIn, Martindale-Hubbell Connected, Legal OnRamp, Ning	Will support blog and Twitter feeds, as well as feed from archive sites (e.g., Facebook/JD Supra widget)
Archiving and Sharing Sites	Stores, shares, and redistributes documents, video, slides, and other information, and allows for embedding at websites and blogs	JD Supra, Docstoc, Scribd, YouTube, SlideShare	Embed feature allows easy display at blogs and websites
Online/Offline Hybrids	Facilitate offline communication and get-togethers through online central location	Biznik, Meetup.com, Twitter (Tweet-ups)	Mixture between online and offline world

Below, we'll discuss the characteristics of each category in detail and give examples of sites within these categories and a few more advanced features that can power charge your use. In the Appendix, you'll also find screenshots of most of these social media sites. Once you've familiarized yourself with these sites, you can move on to Part III, which offers tips on choosing a suite of social media tools that will fit your practice and, most importantly, shows you how to accomplish a variety of professional goals through using social media. For information on creating profiles, move ahead to Part IV on best practices.

The Big Three

Lawyers are a diverse lot, so it's difficult to identify a one-size-fits-all social media application that will serve all lawyers' goals. If pressed, however, we'd choose LinkedIn, Facebook, and Twitter as the "big three" of social media because of their high traffic numbers and, more importantly, their diverse user base, from Fortune 500 corporations (LinkedIn) to small business and consumers (Facebook) to traditional media, start-ups, and high-tech (Twitter). (*See* Chart in Ch. 1 for statistics.) Though second in traffic numbers to first-ranked Facebook, we don't include MySpace in the "big three" because its users are less varied: 72 percent are under the age of 35, with many involved in the music or entertainment industry. For lawyers who target younger clients or represent musicians or artists, MySpace makes sense. (For example, Paul Gardner, an entertainment lawyer in Baltimore, Maryland, landed several high-profile clients through a MySpace presence. (See *Law Practice Today*, March 2008 online at **http://www.abanet.org/lpm/lpt/articles/mkt03081.shtml**). But it's not a platform suitable for a broad range of lawyers.

Participating in the big three gives you coverage in three of the social media categories just described—communications, directory, and community—and thus, diversifies your presence. Second, all of these sites are extremely easy to set up and offer a good way for new users to test the social media waters. Third, you're likely to find that many of your contacts are already using these sites, particularly Facebook and LinkedIn, so you'll have a built-in bunch of folks to connect with right from the start.

One last site bears mention along with the "big three." For lawyers who focus their practice on consumer clients and small business, Avvo, a directory/client review site, will help boost visibility in search engines and has produced leads and paying clients for many lawyers (though results may vary by practice area and geographic location). Avvo is not without controversy because of its rating system for lawyers; so before setting up a profile, take the time to understand how the site works so that you can use it effectively. (*See infra* on page 34 for fuller discussion of Avvo.) Justia's Lawyer Listing (lawyers.justia.com) offers a similar profile as Avvo without the ratings, but it generates less than half of Avvo's monthly traffic. See Compete.com analysis (**http://siteanalytics.compete.com/lawyers.justia.com+www.avvo.com/**).

Directories and Profiles

Characteristics of Directories and Profiles

You may wonder why we've included a directory in a book on social media tools. After all, a directory conjures up visions of a phone book or Martindale-Hubbell: a static listing of basic information.

Welcome to the twenty-first century! Today's next-generation directories offer much more than a basic listing of information. Instead, today's profile sites function as online resumes on steroids. Directory sites enable users to upload biographical information, including employment history, schools attended, association membership, speaking presentations, and publications to their profiles, with live links to all of the information included. The live links make lawyers' past presentations and writings readily accessible to site visitors. And directories can facilitate connections by enabling users to locate others with shared school or employment history.

In contrast to traditional websites, which are one-dimensional, social media profiles support feedback from others. Most profiles encourage lawyers to seek recommendations and endorsements from colleagues and clients or provide a platform where colleagues or clients can provide unsolicited testimonials. Some directories go a step farther and rate lawyers based on input and comments by colleagues and the public.

In addition, most directory sites now include added features to help those who are listed to stand out from the crowd. Sites like Avvo and LinkedIn give registrants the ability to answer users' questions, which can increase the visibility of an online profile and give viewers a peak at a lawyer's expertise and writing skills. Many directory sites also automatically display blog and Twitter feeds so that viewers can learn about a lawyer's writing or interests without having to exit the directory.

General Directories

LinkedIn

LinkedIn: The Basics   LinkedIn is a free online directory and professional networking site that has a membership of more than 50 million professionals from around the world, representing 150 industries.[1] Its primary goal is to increase business opportunities for members by providing them with the ability to connect to potential clients, employees, employers, and other members of their profession. LinkedIn allows users to set up profiles listing job experience, schools attended, and other biographical information.

To access most of the content on LinkedIn, you'll need to register to use it. You can do so at the front page of LinkedIn.com. (See Figure 4-1 below.)

---

[1] http://blog.linkedin.com/2009/10/14/linkedin-50-million-professionals-worldwide/

Figure 4-1. LinkedIn's home page.

Once you've registered, you can set up a profile for yourself (see Part IV). In addition, you'll also need to register and log in to access LinkedIn's search features to find colleagues or identify key players in your practice area. The screenshot below shows how a LinkedIn profile appears once you're logged in to the site. The search bar is on the upper right-hand corner of the page, but you can also use the menu bar to navigate the site.

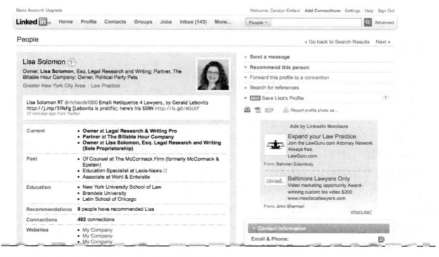

Figure 4-2. LinkedIn's toolbar and search feature.

Even a simple listing on LinkedIn can offer many valuable opportunities for lawyers, including the ability to network with other legal professionals and with potential clients. In addition, it creates enhanced search-engine visibility because lawyers who register profiles at LinkedIn receive the residual benefits of LinkedIn's enormous traffic, and thus often find that their LinkedIn listing boosts their search-engine visibility on Google.

As of November 2008, LinkedIn has allowed companies to create pages containing information about the company, not just the individual [*see* **http://www.linkedin.com/companies?didentcompy**]. Company pages include information about its specialties and list key statistics, such as number of employees, year founded, and location. Lawyers who run several businesses (such as a law practice and consulting firm) may find that the company feature enables them to retain separate identities for multiple ventures.

Figure 4-3. Example of a company site.

LinkedIn: Advanced Features

Beyond creation of a basic profile, LinkedIn offers two more advanced features for lawyers to network and interact. The first is to take advantage of the LinkedIn Group feature and join existing groups that interest you. You can participate in the group forums and interact with other members of the group by asking questions, starting a discussion, or posting a news item of interest. You

> **FACTOID #4**
>
> Eighty percent of companies use LinkedIn as a primary tool to find employees.[2]

[2] http://socialnomics.net/2009/08/11/statistics-show-social-media-is-bigger-than-you-think/

may also discover that other users will find your group through LinkedIn's search features and will ask to join, thus expanding your circle of contacts.

Figure 4-4. To access the "Groups" and "Answers" features discussed below, log onto LinkedIn. You'll see a screen like this one above. Groups are located in the menu bar next to the LinkedIn logo, while "Answers" are located under the "more" menu item.

To join or create a group, click on the "Group" button in the menu bar (see previous diagram) to access the below drop-down menu:

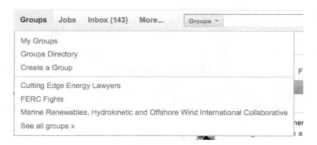

Figure 4-5. LinkedIn's "Groups" drop-down menu.

The Groups Directory option enables you to find a group that suits your interests. Alternatively, by selecting "Create a Group," you can form your own and invite others to join. The groups that you've created will appear in the drop-down menu as well (the above groups were created by Carolyn Elefant, one of this book's authors).

Participating in LinkedIn's question and answers feature provides a second way to build presence on LinkedIn. You can access the LinkedIn Q&A page by hitting the "Answers Button" underneath the "More Button" on the top menu of each page. (See Figure 4-6.) The Q&A page offers users an opportunity to ask questions, respond to questions on specific topics, and even to subscribe to an RSS feed of questions instead of visiting the site to check in. As you answer more questions, you can gain more recognition within the site.

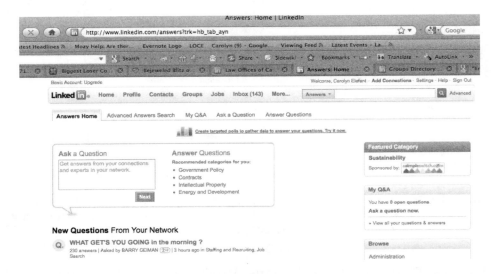

Figure 4-6. LinkedIn's Answers page, which users access through the "Answers Button" under the "More Button."

Lawyer-Related Directories

In addition to a directory like LinkedIn, which supports all users, there are several free online lawyer directories. A few of the most prominent online lawyer directories are Avvo (**http://www.avvo.com/search/search_for_claim_profile**), and the Justia and Legal Information Institute at Cornell Law School legal directory (**https://lawyers.justia.com/signup**).

Avvo
Avvo: The Basics   The first directory, Avvo, is a website that profiles and rates lawyers. One of Avvo's stated goals is to provide "open access to information about lawyers, coupled with guidance on how to use that information. . ." More likely than not, Avvo has already created your bare-bones profile based on public information readily available online from various sources, including state courts, bar associations, and lawyer web-

sites. The basic profile created by Avvo also includes information about lawyers' disciplinary history. Where state bar records (the source of Avvo's information) show a disciplinary violation, a red warning box and/or a notation stating that "this lawyer has been cited for professional misconduct" will appear alongside the lawyer's profile. The information is displayed whether a lawyer claims his profile or not.

If you choose to use online lawyer directories, it makes sense to claim your profile (we describe how to claim your profile in Part IV), which will give you an opportunity to enhance it with relevant, up-to-date information about jobs, cases and articles that you've written, and increase your Avvo rating in the process. You can also invite colleagues to provide endorsements and clients to post reviews about your service.

By adding this information, you have plenty to gain. Avvo is a well-traveled website with great search engine visibility. You will find that you regularly receive communications from potential clients who discovered you as a result of your Avvo profile.

Figure 4-7. How an Avvo profile is displayed for a viewer.

Avvo Advanced Features: Legal Guides and Q&A Avvo offers lawyers two additional features to interact with potential clients and increase visibility on the site. First, lawyers can create legal guides that offer information on legal issues such as immigration, leases, family law, and other topics of interest to consumer clients. Second, lawyers can respond to questions posted by site visitors.

The guides and Q&A features show clients your expertise and, further, give them insight into the approach that you might take in a particular case. In addition, lawyers who write guides or respond to questions earn points, which can lead to a "featured contributor" designation.

One piece of advice: don't be so avid to rack up points that you respond to questions on legal issues arising in states where you don't practice. Doing so could raise potential claims of unauthorized practice of law—particularly from justifiably disgruntled competitors upset by lawyers from another jurisdiction encroaching on their turf. Likewise, while you certainly can't be expected to respond to questions with detailed advice without knowing all of the facts, you should refrain from posting canned answers like "It is impossible to respond without more information, but you should seek legal counsel." Restating the obvious over and over mucks up the site and diminishes its value both for consumers and participants. As is true with much of social media, what counts most is the quality of the interactions, not the quantity.

Avvo: The Controversy   Though we've both claimed our profiles on Avvo, some lawyers choose not to either because of concerns that they

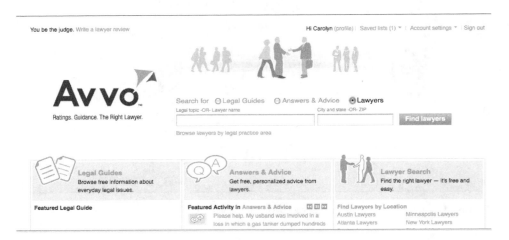

Figure 4-8. What you'll see when you log into your Avvo account. You can access information for writing "Legal Guides" or the "Answers and Advice" by clicking on these topics in the center of the page.

might receive a low rating or that disgruntled clients might post negative reviews. With respect to ratings, most lawyers find that creating a robust profile will allow them to capture an above average rank right off the bat. Adding endorsements from colleagues can also boost ratings, though as discussed in Part IV, deceptive or "reciprocal endorsements" (e.g., you compliment me, I'll compliment you) raise ethics concerns. Moreover, even if these steps don't produce a perfect "10," most clients don't care about the number *per se* but rather, about your actual accomplishments as described in your profile. Just as a consumer looking for a restaurant in a new city will read what others have said and not simply rely on the number of stars received, potential clients will do the same when reviewing lawyers.

Regarding concerns about comments from disgruntled clients, as we mentioned in *Busting the Myths*, most consumers post positive reviews on product rating sites: they *want* to reward a provider or pass on helpful information to other consumers. Moreover, disgruntled clients don't need Avvo to post negative reviews—there's nothing to stop them from doing so at more general sites like Yelp, or even setting up their own blog or website devoted to attacking a lawyer.

Certainly Avvo isn't for everyone. In evaluating which tools are appropriate for your professional goals (see Part III), you may decide that Avvo doesn't make the cut. But if Avvo holds potential value for your practice, don't reflexively rule it out because of concerns about the rankings or client comments.

Justia

Justia is another useful lawyer-only directory, provided in conjunction with Legal Information Institute at Cornell Law School.

The Justia directory is unique in that it allows users to receive "karma credit" and thus higher listings in return for providing free legal information on blogs, wikis, and forums and/or supporting organizations that provide free legal information, like Cornell's Legal Information Institute.

The Justia directory receives a lot of traffic from consumers seeking legal information, advice, and representation. As a result, you can expect to receive regular inquiries through this directory, especially if you are able to increase your "karma" levels.

Figure 4-9. Screenshot of Carolyn Elefant's Justia profile.

Communication and Information Dissemination

A second category of social media sites enables lawyers to disseminate information on a regular, continuously updated basis (as with blogs) or even in realtime (as with Twitter).

Blogs

Blogs are an unparalleled tool for lawyers who enjoy educating clients, indulging in intellectual discourse with colleagues, or staying on top of information. One of the most effective ways to establish an online presence and showcase your legal knowledge is to start a blog. Legal blogs are considered by many to be the cornerstone of a law firm's successful online presence. In fact, in Chapter 9, we'll highlight the versatility of blogging by showing how you can convert and repurpose a series of posts into a presence on six different social media platforms. Still, blogging is effective only if you enjoy the process of writing and can commit to making regular posts, at least one per week, to your blog.

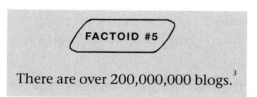

FACTOID #5

There are over 200,000,000 blogs.[3]

If the very idea of maintaining a legal blog makes you groan, then it's entirely possible that blogging is not compatible with your interests or

---

[3] http://socialnomics.net/2009/08/11/statistics-show-social-media-is-bigger-than-you-think/

your personality. That's perfectly fine—there are then other forms of social networking that may be a better fit for you and your law practice. However, if you enjoy writing, you can set up a blog rather easily through the use of services such as Typepad.com or Wordpress.com. Another option is to seek the assistance of a company that sets up and designs legal blogs, such as Justia.com, G2webmedia.com, or Lexblog.com.

Legal blogs can easily serve as the anchor for your online presence and are a very effective way to market your law practice. Blogs are the perfect medium through which you can showcase your expertise and increase your law firm's rankings in search engine results.

The reason for this is simple: search engines seek out and rank higher websites that (1) provide relevant content, (2) are frequently linked to by other websites, and (3) are updated regularly. Blogs satisfy all three of these requirements.

> "Much of what's effective in social media is a natural extension of what an attorney is already doing, and doesn't add nearly so much time as popular wisdom seems to suggest. For instance, most lawyers read legal journals, practice management columns, or case updates; when you see one that's interesting, take thirty seconds to Tweet it, quote from it or add it to a LinkedIn group. If you're going to a local CLE, take your laptop along and Tweet a few gems from the presentation or summarize a key point in a blog post. You'll not only be staying connected, but enhancing your reputation through the valuable information you pass along. Integrating social media into your daily routine doesn't necessarily require a significant time commitment, just a good strategy."
>
> —*Kevin Chern, Esq., President, Total Attorneys*

As you blog, you will naturally use relevant keywords when focusing on subjects relevant to your areas of practice. Possible subjects to blog about include recent events, relevant news stories, posts from other blogs, or newly decided cases. Engage in conversation with other legal bloggers and link to their content when you discuss it. Most likely, those bloggers will soon return the favor by linking to your blog as well.

Once you've started blogging, you can increase traffic to your blog by promoting your blog posts on other social media platforms, including Facebook, LinkedIn, and Twitter. (See Chapter 9, pages 109–110.)

You can learn more about blogging at one of these links:

- http://nylawblog.typepad.com/suigeneris/2007/05/how_to_generate.html
- http://socialmedialawstudent.com/social-media/10-tips-for-starting-your-law-blog/
- http://www.legalmarketingblawg.com/2009/05/blogging-for-lawyers-part-i.html
- http://www.law.com/jsp/legaltechnology/pubArticleLT.jsp?id=1202426527551
- http://www.legalandrew.com/2007/03/27/how-to-start-a-legal-blog/
- http://solosmallfirmblog.typepad.com/mdbartalk/2003/11/so_what_can_web.html

Is Social Media Use Worthwhile If You Don't Have a Blog? [Compiled by Nicole Black.]

(The following is an edited excerpt of a conversation on Twitter about the role of blogs as part of a law firm's online presence.)

- nikiblack: ->@GrantGriffiths You recently said social media is tool to promote a blog & that blogs are not a social media tool. Not sure I agree—that's simply one way to use social media & blogs.
- GrantGriffiths: A blog should be at the center of your Web presence. Social networking tools are just that, tools to grow your blog.
- nikiblack: But blogs don't work for everyone. Some don't like to write. Social media can still work for them & be their online presence.
- GrantGriffiths: Blogging doesn't mean you have to write a law review article every time you touch the keyboard. . .
- GrantGriffiths: You can not totally engage nor build trust with your target audience on social networking tools alone like twitter or facebook.
- nikiblack: I'm all for blogging, but don't think it works for everyone. Preferably, it's the anchor of a Web presence, but that's not necessary.

- JayFleischman: An online presence without a content generation mentality is doomed to failure. Period.
- DisabilityGuy: @nikiblack @GrantGriffiths Social Media helps blog, but not only reason to use social media.
- uMCLE: Agree w/@GrantGriffiths that blog as base for social networking optimal but like @DisabilityGuy can be effect & not cause of social networking.
- DisabilityGuy: Every Facebook LinkedIn & Twitter friend doesn't read blog, but I can still influence on social media.
- JayFleischman: Only if they see you, Steven. Blog gets them in, social media keeps them in your sphere.
- nikiblack: Not everyone enjoys writing-it's a chore for some. Can be detrimental if not good at it.
- uMCLE: Some of my most meaningful relationships on Facebook don't blog and don't have to.
- JayFleischman: But aren't we speaking about professional development, not personal?
- DisabilityGuy: Hard for me to separate professional development from personal. As attorney, personal leads to professional.
- DisabilityGuy: Ideally agree w/@nikiblack should use social media and blog, but not sure one is more important than other. Both work.
- JayFleischman: True, but why engage in activities that are less effective? Tangentially, maybe.
- nikiblack: Because different personalities are more suited to different social media mediums-No reason to force it.

In addition, see Appendix A for the "Ten-Step Countdown to Starting a Blog."

Twitter

Another platform that is seeing a huge amount of growth is Twitter (twitter.com). Many consider it to be one of the most promising professional networking resources available. Given Twitter's uniqueness, it's tough to pigeonhole it into any category. But we believe that it appropriately fits within Communication because that's one of Twitter's primary purposes. Plus, Twitter is frequently described as a microblog, so it makes sense to group it in the same category as blogs.

Twitter is a free, Web-based communications platform that allows users to share information with others who have similar personal and professional interests. Users communicate using text-based posts ("tweets") of up to 140 characters in length. After signing up, you can locate others with similar interests or backgrounds through "Twitter lists" or a directory, such as Twellow (twellow.com), then follow them and reply to Twitter posts. Tweets from users who you follow will appear next to a small photo in your personal timeline, which are visible to you when you log into your Twitter page (*see* screenshot, NikiBlack profile below). Note: most Twitter users don't access the site directly from the Web, but instead opt to use applications like Tweetdeck to organize Twitter streams, or Tweetie.com to access Twitter from a phone. See page 148–149 for discussion of these applications and see Appendix B for a Twitter glossary.

It is estimated that Twitter currently has more than 18 million accounts registered and its user base is expanding quickly. The projected number of users for 2010 is 26 million, or 15.5 percent of adult Internet users.[4]

Companies, government agency staff members, and individuals use Twitter in a variety of unique ways, which are constantly evolving. For example, large businesses use Twitter to provide information to their customers and,

Figure 4-10. Screenshot of @NikiBlack's Twitter profile. The center bar shows Niki's tweets to friends or followers, while the sidebar lists the number of friends or followers. You can see who Niki follows or is following by clicking on the "following" or "followers" link in the right sidebar.

---

[4]**http://mashable.com/2009/09/14/twitter-2009-stats/**

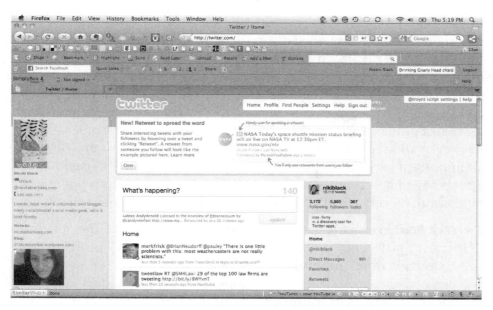

Figure 4-11. This screenshot shows the view that a user sees when logging into a Twitter account. To send a tweet, enter a 140-character message in the "What's happening?" space.

occasionally, personalized customer service. President Barack Obama's presidential campaign used Twitter to connect with and update supporters. News outlets, such as the BBC and CNN, use Twitter to rapidly disseminate breaking news.

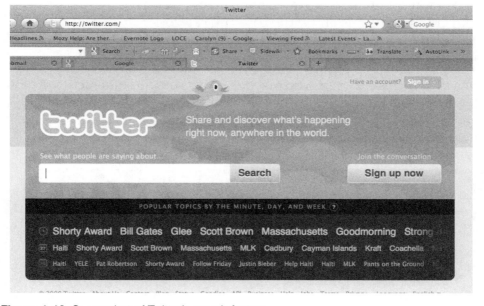

Figure 4-12. Screenshot of Twitter's search feature.

In some cases, news breaks on Twitter before the major news outlets report on it, which happened during an earthquake in California in 2009. California-based Twitter users were the first to "tweet" about the earthquake as they experienced it. Similarly, Twitter played an instrumental role in the dissemination of information surrounding the Iran elections and subsequent protests, after the Iranian government barred traditional journalist outlets from reporting the events that occurred. Some judges have even allowed journalists to live tweet from the courtroom. Twitter is an important social media platform that lawyers should not overlook. That being said, it is not ideal for all lawyers. But for certain types of practices, it can be very effective, as we will discuss in the chapters that follow.

Twitter Features and Basics   Twitter offers several unique features of interest to lawyers. First, Twitter allows users to set up a profile with 140 characters worth of information. You'd be surprised at how much you can convey within those limitations. Second, Twitter lets users search conversations in realtime using its built-in search function which is like putting a fine tuner on the pulse of the Web.

Additionally, as discussed in Chapter 8, the search function offers important competitive intelligence capability. You can access the Twitter search feature right on the home page, **www.twitter.com**. Alternatively, some of the management tools for Twitter, like **www.tweetdeck.com**, discussed below, also include a search feature.

Finally, Twitter recently introduced lists, which are curated by users. Lists offer a way for others to view recommendations of a user or to follow certain groups of people on Twitter based on categories created by other Twitter users.

There are many law-related lists that were curated by Twitter users, some of which include lawyers who practice law in your area of practice. By following these lists, you will be able to track discussions between lawyers about some of the latest decisions and issues that affect your areas of practice. A number of law-related Twitter lists can be found in the sidebar.

Links to a Sampling of Law-related Lists

- **Bankruptcy Lawyers:** http://twitter.com/JayFleischman/bankruptcy-lawyers
- **Criminal Law Attorneys:** http://www.twitter.com/nikiblack/criminal-law-attorneys

- **eDiscovery:** http://twitter.com/AdvertisingLaw/ediscovery
- **Employment Law:** http://twitter.com/CJMcKinney/employment law
- **Housing Law UK:** http://twitter.com/HousingBenefit/housing-law-uk
- **Internet Law:** http://twitter.com/macgill/internetlaw
- **Legal News:** http://twitter.com/AdvertisingLaw/legal-news
- **Legal Tech Thinkers:** http://twitter.com/nikiblack/legal-tech-thinkers

You can discover other law-related Twitter lists through Listorious (listorious.com), which provides a directory of Twitter lists. To locate law-related lists, simply search for "law" or "legal."

You can also add Twitter lists to your RSS feed reader, thus making it easier for you to track the conversations relevant to your practice by using the tool Twitter Lists 2 RSS (**www.twiterlist2rss.appspot.com**).

A Conversation on Twitter as a Tool for Lawyers

(The following is an edited conversation from Twitter regarding whether Twitter is useful for lawyers.)

- nikiblack: Twitter is the most important SM platform right now . . . but am not sure that Twitter is best format for many lawyers
- DisabilityGuy: Twitter is important to lawyers for learning new things. May not directly drive business, but helps lawyers practice better
- nikiblack: That's a great point-for lawyers—Twitter is better as an RSS reader, info. gatherer & for networking, too
- uMCLE: When attys need to become "experts" overnight, use social media: Twitter for current issues/language then LinkedIn for depth
- DisabilityGuy: True value is indirect marketing opportunities. Twitter presence provides visibility, may lead 2 new client
- LeighMonette: I met with 2 clients a few days ago who found me through my tweets. I use primarily for networking though

♦ LeighMonette: @ I agree re: indirect mktg. Engaging in meaning-ful exchanges with peers helps me connect and show ability.

♦ uMCLE: Of all platforms, real-time exchange that Twitter offers mimic traditional relationship building, but what's truly unique is the unprecedented access from and to potential clients

♦ LeighMonette: Real-time is a definite plus, but can cut both ways if you're not always in the stream. . .

♦ DisabilityGuy: Another viewpoint to add-this article: Are Lawyers Getting Clients From Twitter? **http://twurl.nl/fud4le**

Archiving and Storage Sites

Overview

Archiving sites let users upload content to the Web and redistribute it in the same format. For example, when you upload a pleading to a site like JD Supra, users can view it in the same format in which you filed it with the court. The same is true for sites like SlideShare, which lets users share slides created using PowerPoint or similar programs, and YouTube, a site for sharing video content. As we'll discuss later in the book, sharing doc-uments online forwards any number of legitimate reasons for engaging in social media, including showcasing one's expertise and increasing your law firm's standing in search engine results.

In addition to redistributing content in the same format in which it is provided (thus making sharing easier since users don't need to convert files), archiving sites share several other common features. First, they enable users to embed the documents within a blog, website, or Facebook page so that readers can view it there instead of having to backtrack to the archive site. Second, archiving sites enable comments where viewers can offer feedback on slide presentations, videos, or writings. Many find the constructive comments to be very helpful and use the feedback to improve presentations and materials moving forward.

Finally, most archive sites have powerful tagging features, which enable viewers to categorize videos or documents and make them searchable. Given the large volume of traffic at many of these sites, use of the tag-ging feature will make your document or video easier to locate and increase your SEO. Increasingly, users are turning to archiving sites as stand-alone search engines; instead of going to Google, they are search-ing these sites directly for information. In fact, YouTube is the second most popular online search engine after Google.[5] That alone is reason enough to explore use of these sites.

Specific Sites

YouTube is the largest video-sharing website and more than a billion views of videos on its site occur every day.[6] Vimeo (**www.vimeo.com**) and Viddler (**www.viddler.com**) are emerging competitors in this market as well and are becoming increasingly popular. All of these sites allow users to embed videos uploaded to the site elsewhere onto other social networks, including Twitter, Facebook, and blogs. Generally speaking, lawyers have been slow to embrace this particular form of social networking, but you can expect the reluctance to engage with this platform to decline as online video sharing becomes increasingly ubiquitous.

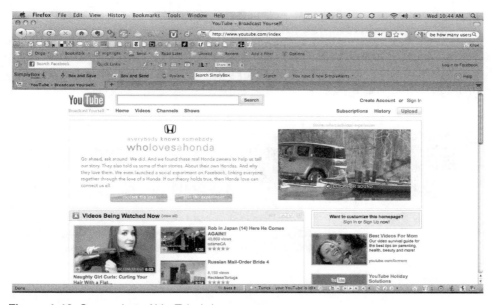

Figure 4-13. Screenshot of YouTube's home page.

For lawyers, video sharing presents a particularly appealing alternative to more static (not to mention more costly) online television advertising. Many of today's lawyer-produced YouTube videos have a primary purpose of educating clients rather than soliciting them. For example, New York medical malpractice attorney Gerry Oginski has prepared a series of dozens of videos explaining how certain aspects of the legal process work. Whereas producing education-based video for television may not have

[5] **http://socialnomics.net/2009/08/11/statistics-show-social-media-is-bigger-than-you-think/**
[6] **http://en.wikipedia.org/wiki/YouTube (11/09).**

been effective, given the high cost of ads, and television audiences' short attention spans, the format works well for the Internet.

SlideShare (**www.slideshare.com**) bills itself as a "business media site for sharing presentations, documents and PDFs." It receives 23 million visitors per month.[7] After uploading a slide deck used in a presentation, you can then embed and share your work, the slide decks that you have created, on Twitter, blogs, Facebook and other social networking sites. (See discussion on page 70 for examples of embedded content.) In other words, you can insert the slide shows into blog posts, on a website, or onto your profile on social networking sites like Facebook. This is a very effective way to showcase an area of expertise because it makes people aware of the fact that you are speaking at legal conferences about specific topics. Moreover, posting slides allows you to get more mileage out of a speaking engagement because you can make content available to those who didn't attend your presentation.

For example, Nicole Black, one of the authors of this book, uploaded a slide show to SlideShare and, two weeks later, the presentation had received over 1,100 views.[8]

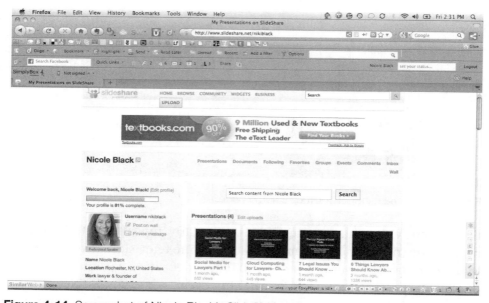

Figure 4-14. Screenshot of Nicole Black's SlideShare page.

---

[7] http://www.slideshare.net/about

[8] http://www.slideshare.net/nikiblack/6-things-lawyers-should-know

Scribd (**www.scribd.com**) is one of the largest document sharing sites. It provides a publishing platform that allows users to upload and share original writings and documents. Scribd is a free service and is used by many large publishing companies to distribute content, including *The New York Times*, *The Chicago Tribune,* and Simon & Schuster.[9] Of course, when uploading any client documents to the Internet, care should be taken to redact client names and any other confidential information.

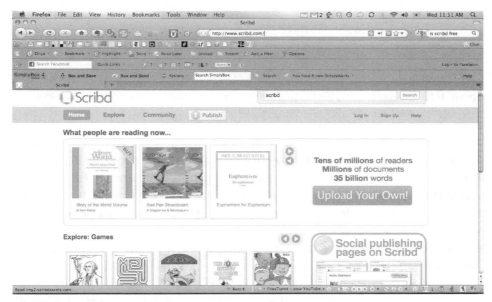

Figure 4-15. Screenshot of Scribd's home page.

Another document sharing site is Docstoc (**www.docstoc.com**), which allows users to create a profile and upload and share all types of business documents, including legal, business, financial, technical, and educational documents. Some documents can be accessed for free, while others are only accessible if you pay for a premium membership. You can tag documents with relevant terms to make them find-able both within Docstoc as well as through Google. As with SlideShare, which allows users to embed slides within a website, Docstoc and Scribd offer the same feature for uploaded documents (*see* discussion, *infra* re: Convergence).

---

[9] **http://www.scribd.com/about**

Figure 4-16. Example of a Docstoc profile. Documents uploaded by a user are listed in the right column, with tags and categories listed underneath.

Finally, JD Supra (**www.jdsupra.com**) is an online platform that allows you to showcase your expertise by uploading and sharing your legal work product. You can distribute and showcase filings, decisions, articles, newsletters, blog entries, presentations, and media coverage. Once you've done so, JD Supra makes it easy to distribute the content to any profiles you've already set up on LinkedIn, Facebook, and, if applicable, Twitter. Use of the platform is free for individual lawyers and law students, and also offers varying levels of membership for lawyers and law firms.

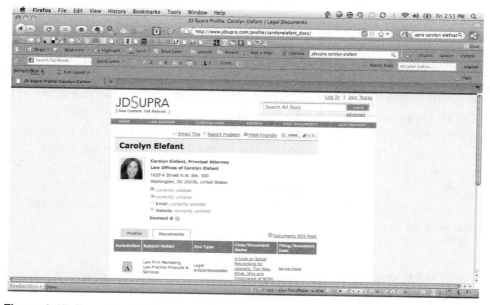

Figure 4-17. Example of JD Supra profile.

Attorneys should be pairing their networking with content publication. It is impossible to engender professional trust without showing your work product. JDSupra is a great way to take content you may have already developed elsewhere and place it in a searchable database available to potential clients and other lawyers.

—Martha Sperry, Associate Claims Counsel for OneBeacon Insurance Group; Principal, Advantage Associates; Massachusetts.

Communities: Professional and Personal

General Overview
Community sites give lawyers a chance to interact and build relationships. Currently, there are two categories of community sites available for lawyers: general sites like Facebook, as well as lawyer-specific sites like Martindale-Hubbell Connected. Surprisingly, at least thus far, it is sites like Facebook that hold the most appeal for lawyers.

Facebook
Facebook (facebook.com), likely the most well known of the three networking sites, originally launched as a social network for college students, but was opened to the public in September 2006. Facebook currently has over 300 million active users and its fastest growing demographic is people over 35 years of age.[10] While many think of it as a predominantly social networking site, it can provide valuable professional networking opportunities for lawyers.

Facebook is a global social networking site that allows anyone to join. Individual lawyers can connect with people they know, including those with whom they have lost contact. In other words, after creating a simple profile in a matter of minutes, a lawyer can connect with virtually everyone from her past, including former classmates, long-lost relatives—you name it. The platform also is quite good at locating people you may know based on the people with whom you already have a connection. Facebook lets you interact with your friends by posting comments on their "wall," uploading photos, or sending private messages.

---

[10] **http://en.wikipedia.org/wiki/Facebook (11/09).**

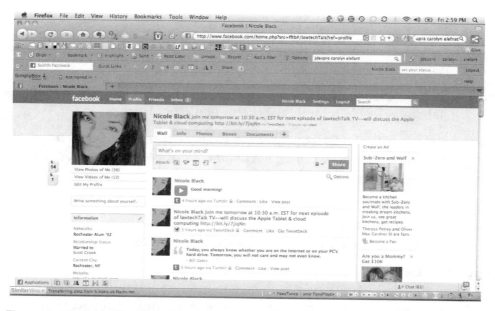

Figure 4-18. Nicole Black's Facebook profile. The status bar in the center of the profile lets users provide a status update on what they're doing. The updates appear on the user's profile and friends can post comments or replies using the "comment" feature that appears below the updates. All of this communication appears on what is known as the user's "wall."

Why is Facebook a good thing for lawyers? Because every lawyer has a long-lost network that spans the globe! People who know you but have lost track of you over time now will know you're an lawyer. You will receive messages from old friends and from relatives seeking legal counsel—either for themselves or on behalf of a friend in your town.

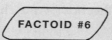

If Facebook were a country it would be the world's fourth largest between the United States and Indonesia (note that Facebook is now creeping up and recently announced 300 million users).[11]

In addition, because of its more casual tone, Facebook is analogous to business development activities like golf, ballgames, or a wine tasting: all are enjoyable activities, unrelated to law, that enable lawyers and their clients to get to know each other on a personal level and in doing so, determine whether they can work well together. It's well known that we prefer to work with those with whom we like to spend time. Facebook

---

[11] **http://socialnomics.net/2009/08/11/statistics-show-social-media-is-bigger-than-you-think/**

provides a chance to build an out-of-the-office relationship in a more casual environment.

Likewise, Facebook serves as a great adjunct for many of our professional activities. For example, there's no better way to gain visibility and make yourself popular than by serving as the designated "photographer" at bar association events and posting the photos to Facebook. Facebook offers a feature called "tagging" which lets you identify each person in a photo.

Figure 4-19. When a Facebook photo is posted to an album, you can identify the people in the photo by using the "Tag This Photo" feature in the right column under the photo.

Of course, mixing business with pleasure also has its risks. For example, let's say a buddy posts a photo of you from your college days, slumped over a table in the bar and tags you. That photo will be visible to all of your friends, including all clients or professional colleagues whom you've "friended" and, needless to say, may not make the best impression. Likewise, even if you're scrupulous about what *you* post on your wall, you have little control over what friends post—which may include profanity or other language that a client may find offensive. True, you can remove the comments, but by that time, others may have seen them so the damage will already be done.

For lawyers using Facebook for business and personal matters, we recommend several precautions to avoid making a poor or unprofessional impression. First, some lawyers can limit access to personal information by simply not "friending" clients, except those with whom they've developed a collegial relationship. For lawyers who want to maintain a less formal relationship with clients, consider creating a Fan Page (discussed in the next section) for your law firm. Second, users can also pick and choose the information they want to make publicly available by using Facebook's comprehensive "privacy settings" in creating a profile. With privacy settings, you can separate friends into "personal" and "profession" lists, and limit access to tagged photos or wall posts to personal friends. To learn how to use privacy features, see Part IV, where we discuss setting up a Facebook profile.

Over the last year, lawyers have flocked to Facebook in droves, creating networking groups centered around various areas of practice. Joining and participating in these groups is a cost-free and useful way to meet other lawyers from across the country and reconnect with law school and undergraduate colleagues. Facebook groups include message forums that allow members to discuss topics of their choice with other participants and are a good way to connect and network with other lawyers who have similar interests.

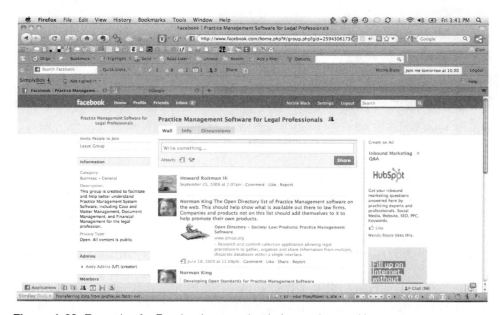

Figure 4-20. Example of a Facebook group that is focused toward lawyers.

Breathing life into those lost connections is priceless, and Facebook is a unique platform that makes it possible. Do not pass up the opportunity to have a presence on this platform.

Facebook Fan Pages

Facebook also allows a business to create a free "Facebook fan page." A Facebook fan page is a public profile that can be used to share business and product information with other Facebook users. Facebook fan pages are a relatively new feature, but as *The New York Times* reported in November 2009, increasingly, small businesses are using them to establish a Web presence and stay in touch with customers.[12]

Fan pages offer similar opportunities for law firms. Law firms can stay on their client's radar by creating an active community around the firm's Facebook fan page, listing education seminars or charitable events that the firm is sponsoring, or simply posting photos and bios of staff. Once you've created a fan page, you can invite other users to become "fans" of the business's fan page. The following is an example of a law-related Facebook fan page:

Figure 4-21. Screenshot of a fan page for Untethered Lawyer, which is a law-related blog on practice management and unbundled legal services.

---

[12] **http://www.nytimes.com/2009/11/12/business/smallbusiness/12guide.html?_r=1**

Another Perspective

A Facebook fan page can be a great way to cross-market other products and services to people with whom you're already connected. Fan pages can be used as an easy way to maintain relationships with past clients, which makes them more likely to return to you for future needs and to refer friends and family. And, the creative attorney can use a fan page for other purposes as well, such as encouraging payment of outstanding balances by offering all fans a 10 percent discount on payments made during a particular time frame or for other business promotions.

—Kevin Chern, Esq., President, Total Attorneys

What Kinds of Tools Work for Lawyers?

(The following is an edited conversation from Twitter regarding the utility of Facebook fan pages for lawyers and law firms.)

♦ nikiblack: Re: Facebook fan pages. I don't see the benefit of fan pages. Am I alone?

♦ TMarieHilton: FB fan pages have potential to be a 'one-stop' shop to combine blog/social media feeds w/personal interaction, but not there yet

♦ advocatesstudio: Value is in helping firm/product you might want to support—the pages on Facebook get good google juice.

♦ davidtcarson: Most fan page requests I receive are from lawyers I'm already following on Twitter. And the fan pages have no unique content.

♦ nikiblack: I don't see FB as an outright biz tool. FB is about personal connections leading to biz-not blatant biz PR

♦ dougcornelius: I just don't know how lawyers and law firms fit into the mix. "Fan" seems like the wrong word.

♦ nikiblack: I get the search end of things—but do more fans increase your SEO at all?

♦ justia: number of fans does lead to higher FB search rankings, but does not impact Google rankings

♦ nikiblack: FB fan pages will work 4 biz that are part of user's social experience-music, movies, celebrities, food/wine, tech products-not service biz

♦ RWSJR: People do business and are source of referrals for those they know or think they know. Properly done FB presence could do this.

♦ nikiblack: Re: FB pages, a lawyer just messaged me and advised that over the last few months she's gotten 3 new clients through her FB fan page.

What About Facebook for Advertising?

Capitalizing on their high traffic statistics, many social media sites like Facebook or LinkedIn offer users the ability to place paid ads. In fact, if you currently use sites like Facebook or LinkedIn, you've probably noticed targeted advertisements that appear on your profile page when you log on to the site.

Advertising on social media sites is attractive for three reasons. The first is traffic and demographics. According to numbers from Nielsen Online, users spent an average of five hours, 46 minutes on Facebook in the month of August. To put that in perspective, that's **triple the amount of time they spent on Google!** (http://mashable .com/2009/09/17/facebook-google-time-spent/) And as mentioned earlier, the 35+ age demographic, one of the most desirable for marketing, also happens to be the largest growing group on social media platforms. In addition, LinkedIn provides a way for lawyers with business-oriented practices to reach other professionals, a feature absent from more consumer-oriented options like Yellow Pages or Craigslist.

Second, social media sites aggregate all kinds of data on users' employment, preference, geographic location, and family status. Thus, it's possible to develop highly focused marketing campaigns that enable you to target your "ideal" clients.

Third, advertising on social media not only costs less than conventional advertising, but also gives users more control over costs. Like Google ads, Facebook and LinkedIn allow you to identify the demographic you want to target, to set a monthly budget for ads, and stop using ads whenever you want. By contrast, the Yellow Pages require lawyers to lock into costly, long-term contacts.

Though ad placement on social media sites may turn out to be an effective marketing technique, strictly speaking, it's not social media. In our view, paid advertising on social media sites more accurately fits within the category of pure marketing or advertising, much the same as using Google ads or advertising in a newspaper or on Craigslist. By contrast, social media involves active engagement and participation in conversations, online relationships and discourse, and as such, is very different from passive advertising.

If you're interested in exploring social media ad placement further, most sites have advertising links where you can gain more information. *See, e.g.,* Facebook (**http://www.facebook.com/advertising/ ?src=pf**) or LinkedIn (**http://www.linkedin.com/static?key= advertising_info&trk=hb_ft_ads**).

The Other Public Social Networks—A Motley Crew

MySpace (myspace.com) is a social network similar to Facebook and has approximately 200 million registered users.[13] The platform is frequented primarily by teenagers and young adults. More than 50 percent of its

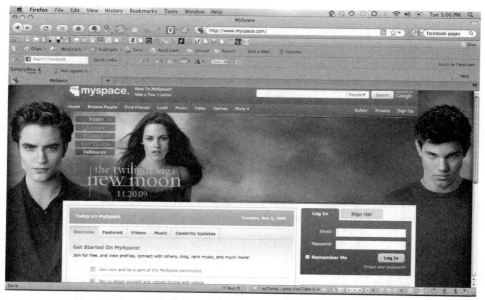

Figure 4-22. Screenshot of MySpace.com home page.

[13]http://wiki.answers.com/Q/How_many_users_does_myspace_have

users are younger than 25 years of age[14] and there are far fewer lawyers participating on this site compared to other social networking sites. For those reasons, MySpace is not a very useful platform for attorneys in regard to the promotion of their practice or networking with other professionals. However, MySpace can be very useful as a tool for locating witnesses or heirs or for obtaining background information about potential clients or opposing parties in litigation.

Plaxo (plaxo.com) is an online address book and social networking site. It connects you with the contacts already in your Outlook or Mac OS X address book and then aggregates the social content that your contacts create at sites like Twitter and Flickr. It also automatically updates the contact information of those with whom you are connected.

Figure 4-23. This is a screenshot of Plaxo's home page.

Naymz (naymz.com) bills itself as a "professional networking platform (that) allows people to find and discover new connections, opportunities, ideas, and information based on their backgrounds and reputations." The platform has over one million registered users and, in many ways, is similar to LinkedIn. Naymz also offers reputation management and monitoring and also provides analytics about those who visit your profile.

---

[14]**http://technomarketer.typepad.com/technomarketer/2009/03/the-age-of-facebook-vs-myspace-februarymarch-edition.html**

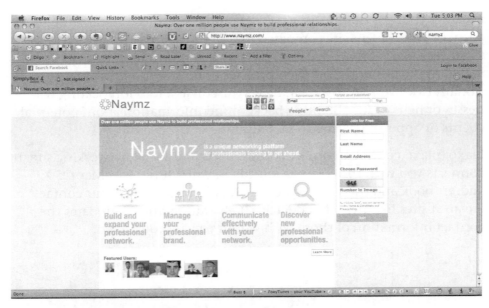

Figure 4-24. This is a screenshot of the home page of Naymz.

Ning (ning.com) is a platform that allows its users to create their own social networks. The networks can be customized to include videos, discussion forums, and events. Although most law firms have not yet ventured into Ning territory, an lawyer networking Ning was recently created and is an example of one way that legal professionals can use this type of platform:

Figure 4-25. This is a screenshot of a networking site for lawyers called "Lawyer Connection," which can be found at (**http://lawyerconnection.ning.com/**).

Second Life (secondlife.com) is the largest, most popular virtual community. It is a platform that allows users to participate in an online virtual reality program. As of October 2009, Second Life had over 16 million registered users.[15] Although the vast majority of lawyers have little experience with Second Life, a few have established virtual law practices within the platform and users have even established the Second Life Bar Association (**www.slba.info**), which holds monthly meetings within the platform and offers CLE classes.

Interestingly, disputes arising on the virtual platform have spilled over into the "real world" and some lawyers are developing a niche practice representing Second Life litigants.[16]

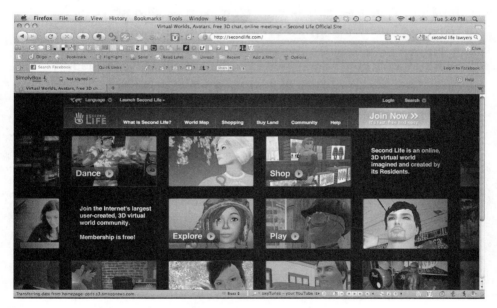

Figure 4-26. This is a screenshot of the main page of Second Life.

Lawyer-Specific Community Sites

Online legal networks

Recently, a number of online networks were created specifically for lawyers. Most of these platforms are limited to lawyers or legal professionals. Some require verification of your status as an lawyer prior to allowing you to participate. In some cases, the verification process can be quite lengthy. All of these networks are free to join.

---

[15] http://en.wikipedia.org/wiki/Second_Life (11/09).
[16] http://www.sfgate.com/cgi-bin/article.cgi?f=/c/a/2009/04/26/BUH0172A42.DTL

The online legal community is divided over the value of these networks. Some think there is minimal value to limiting your networking experience to lawyers-only formats while others believe that a lot can be gained from this type of closed network, including referrals and advice to support your practice from others who practice in the same area of law as you do. As with any type of social media platform, when choosing which platforms to utilize, you need to consider your goals and your comfort level with any given social media platform, as we discuss in Part III.

The Value of Lawyer-Specific Forums

(In a study) that we commissioned on the topic through Leader Networks (**www.leadernetworks.com**), the Networks for Counsel Study, we asked counsel what the advantages were to participating in a legal-only professional network. The top answers included: (1) Facilitates easier exchange of information and experiences between peers; (2) Access to information (not available) elsewhere; (3) More (able to) quickly identify, evaluate, and select outside counsel; (4) Lower costs associated with traditional networking; (5) Ability to increase . . . visibility among peers; and (6) Creates a formal and exclusive forum for professional collaboration.

—John Lipsey, Esq., Vice President,
Corporate Counsel Services, LexisNexis

The first example of a legal network is Legally Minded. Legally Minded (**www.legallyminded.com**) is an online community established by the American Bar Association (ABA) that serves the legal profession. You do not have to be a member of the ABA to join. The site includes interactive group forums, blogs, and wikis.

There are state bar social networking sites as well. For example, the Texas State Bar began a closed social networking site (**https://texasbar.affinity circles.com/sbot/auth/login**) on June 1, 2007, using Affinity Circles, which is a social networking platform. The Texas Bar Circle was the first social networking site created by a bar association, and by the summer of 2009 it had over 10,000 members. Other states, including California, are considering launching similar social networking sites for bar members.

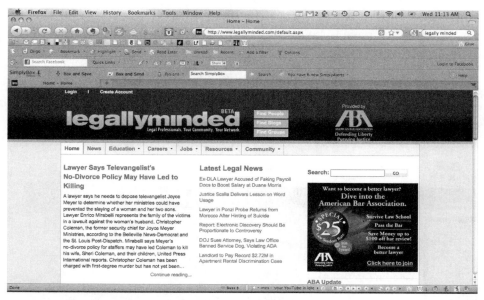

Figure 4-27. Legallyminded's home page.

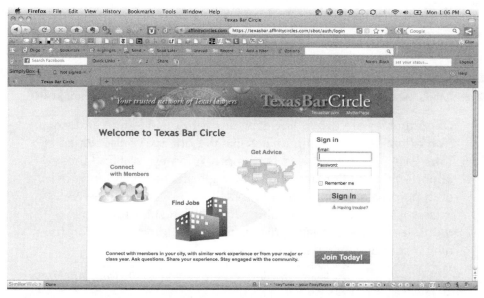

Figure 4-28. This screenshot is the home page of the Texas Bar Circle.

Another useful resource offered by the ABA is the Solosez email listserv (**www.solosez.net**). Although not technically Social Media, this listserv is a great resource for solo lawyers that allows you to interact with and learn from other solos. It is a very active listserv and has well over 2,700 members. You do not have to be a member of the ABA to join the listserv.

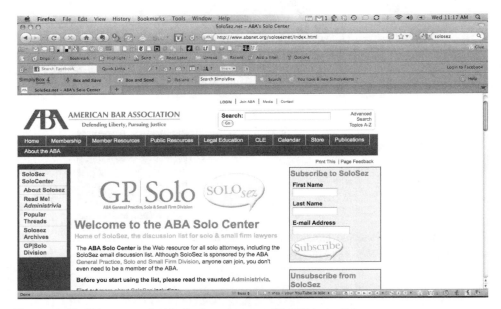

Figure 4-29. This screenshot is the home page of the Solosez listserv.

The Value of Listservs

Opportunities are expanding everyday with the addition and expansion of online legal communities like the one we've developed at Total PMA, industry listservs, and more. Attorneys will find those opportunities by thinking about their specific needs in terms of both practice area and nature of practice. For instance, the NACBA listserv is a great source of information about substantive bankruptcy law, while Solosez provides insights and discussion on running a solo or very small law practice.

—Ed Scanlon, Founder and CEO, Total Attorneys

If you're comfortable with the listserv format, there are other listservs that you can join as well that may provide you with a great resource for your law practice. For example, the New York Association of Criminal Defense Lawyers has a listserv for its members.

Another lawyer-specific site to consider is LawLink (**www.lawlink.com**), a social networking site for the legal community at large. It consists of four separate, but connected networks: an lawyer network, an expert witness network, a law student network, and a law professional network. The site allows you to create and join groups, participate in discussions in forums, and interact with other users of the platform.

Figure 4-30. This screenshot shows the home page of LawLink.

Martindale-Hubbell Connected (**http://www.martindale.com/connected**) is a networking site for legal professionals. This platform is in beta and all of the planned features have not yet been activated. However, the long-term goal is to fully integrate a number of features into the network so that users can take advantage of the Martindale-Hubbell database of more than one million lawyers. Currently, it offers the ability to connect with friends and colleagues, participate in discussion forums, and share article and blog posts within the network.

Prior to joining, you must first provide a fairly detailed amount of information, which is then verified through a stringent process. You are not granted access to the network until your profile has been verified by Martindale-Hubbell. This is done so that members will rest assured that they are interacting in a closed community with independently verified legal professionals.

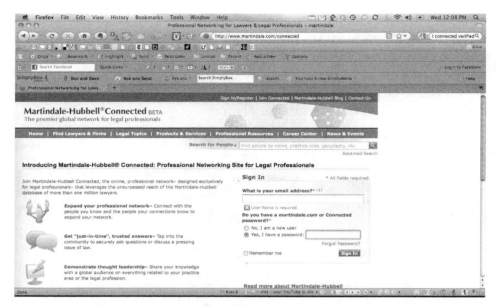

Figure 4-31. This is a screenshot of the login page of Martindale-Hubbell Connected.

Lawyer Connection (**http://lawyerconnection.ning.com/**), which was discussed in the previous section, is an lawyer network created using a Ning platform. Its self-stated mission is "to create a community of lawyers each of whom is dedicated to assisting one other lawyer in making it through the economic downturn." The network has over 200

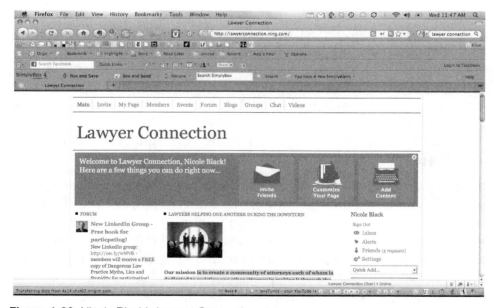

Figure 4-32. Nicole Black's Lawyer Connection page.

members, many of whom are also very active in other online forums, such as Twitter. Members can connect with other members by creating and participating in groups. Members can also post and share articles and blog posts.

Closed and for-fee networks

Though most networks are free and open to anyone who is a lawyer, there are some exceptions. One example of a closed network, Solo Practice University (**www.solopracticeuniversity.com**) is an online educational and networking community for lawyers and law students. Its goal is to provide support to and teach its members how to build their own solo practices. It is a fee-based platform offering virtual classrooms and online forums that allow members to interact with and learn from each other. By way of disclosure, both authors of this book have been instructors at Solo Practice University.

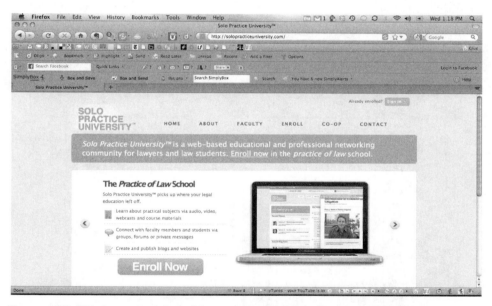

Figure 4-33. This is a screenshot of the main page of Solo Practice University.

Online to Offline Hybrids

Many lawyers fear that social media will lead to a reclusive existence of being holed-up in a home office with nose pressed to the computer screen. Yet the opposite is true: social media is actually encouraging in-person communication; the 2009 Pew Report Study found an increase in personal connection as a result of social media.

It's no surprise that social media facilitates offline connection. One of our favorite aspects of social media is that it serves as an icebreaker, giving folks an opportunity to get to know each other in advance of hitting a networking event or conference. Where once these types of events could be intimidating, they're far more palatable when you can connect with someone you've been eager to meet online instead of aimlessly wandering between the bar and the food table in search of a friendly face. On page 86, we'll offer some specific tips for converting online connections into offline relationships, but for now, we'll share information on sites with the specific purpose of facilitating personal interaction.

Meetup

Meetup describes itself as the world's largest network of local groups. Meetup makes it easy for anyone to organize a local group or find one of the thousands already meeting up face-to-face. More than 2,000 groups get together in local communities each day, each one with the goal of improving themselves or their communities.

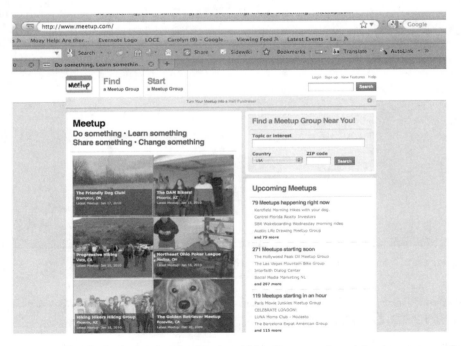

Figure 4-34. This is the login page for Meetup. Using the menu bar at the top, you can find a Meetup group or start one of your own.

Meetup allows users to set up group profiles on its sites and list events. Members can communicate through mailing lists within the site. But ultimately, the purpose of Meetup is to convert the online presence into offline interaction.

Law firms use Meetup in a variety of ways. For example, DLA Piper, a global law firm, is a member of the 4,000-member Silicon Valley NewTech Meetup group and frequently sponsors meetings.[17] One group of lawyers set up a Lunchtime with Lawyers Meetup group to provide a casual setting where business people can get together with lawyers to ask legal questions.

Figure 4-35. Lunchtime with Lawyers group page on Meetup.com.

Finally, smaller local bar associations with few resources can use Meetup as an inexpensive way to organize, by listing members and getting the word out about events.

---

[17]Video discussion describing DLA Piper's sponsorships online at **http://siliconvalley10.cityspur .com/2009/10/01/dla-piper-law-firm-newtech-meetup/**

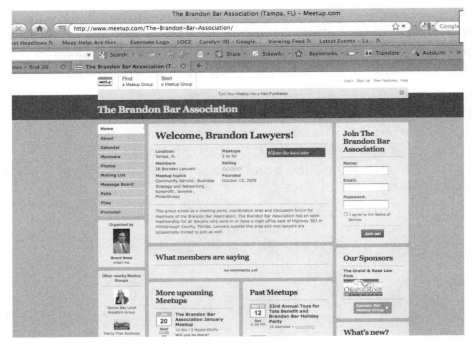

Figure 4-36. The Brandon Bar Association home page.

Tools to Coordinate Your Social Media Presence

With social media use on the rise, and new tools constantly emerging, it can be difficult to keep on top of your social media platforms and coordinate your presence, particularly if you're using a large number of applications. In this section, we discuss three ways to seamlessly coordinate, integrate, and promote your social media presence.

1. Embedding Tools

Social media sites like YouTube, SlideShare.net, and Docstoc include a feature called "embedding," which allows users to post uploaded videos, slides, or documents to their website or blog. By embedding a video or slideshow in a blog, a visitor can view it right there, instead of having to go to YouTube or SlideShare. Embedding is accomplished by cutting and pasting a piece of code generated each time you upload a video or document and pasting it into a blog post or the code for your website.

Figure 4-37. YouTube video embedded in blog post.

You can also embed badges or ratings in your blog. For example, Avvo lets users display a badge showing their Avvo rating at their website or blog. To display a badge, log into your Avvo profile and select "Dashboard." Then, select the "Put Avvo Badge on Your Webpage" button on the right side of the Dashboard page.

Figure 4-38. "Put Avvo Badge on Your Webpage" button at bottom right on Avvo's Dashboard page.

Selecting the badge button will take you to the screen that follows, which displays the code to copy and embed in your blog.

Figure 4-39. Avvo's badge code.

You can copy and paste the code above to place the Avvo badge on the sidebar of your website or blog. Most blog software explains how to embed code in the sidebar to display the badge.

2. Promoting Your Social Media Profile

In order for others to engage with you on social media, they need to know where to find you. Make it easy for colleagues, friends, and existing and potential clients to locate you on social media by promoting your presence across platforms.

For example, list your social media presence on Twitter, Facebook, and LinkedIn at the side of your blog or website. In fact, including a link to LinkedIn on a blog or website obviates the need to include a lengthy biographic description on your blog—readers can just visit your LinkedIn profile.

Another way that you can promote your social media presence is to include links to your social media platforms in the signature bar of your email. You can simply include a text link under your name (e.g., **www.blogofattorneyjones.com**, follow me @attorneyjones234). If you prefer a slightly fancier look, you can set up an online profile box on **www.retaggr.com** and set up your email program to have the Retaggr profile render in your signature block.

Figure 4-40. An example of social media listings at a website. The graphic at right is an enlargement of the "connect with us" feature in the right sidebar.

Figure 4-41. This screenshot shows a Retaggr online profile that the user can include in the email signature block.

PART THREE

Implementing Social Media

CHAPTER FIVE

Choosing Social Media Tools

LAWYERS CAN USE A variety of platforms to accomplish their goals. So how can lawyers decide which platform to use? In this chapter, we'll give you some criteria to guide your decision.

Criteria for Choosing Social Media Platforms

We're not comfortable telling you which social media tools to choose. In fact, each of the authors has her own suite of favorites. Below are some factors to consider.

Geographic Locale
Though social media tools reside online, oddly, some are more popular in certain areas than others. For example, we discovered that Rochester, where one of the authors lives, is a hotbed of Twitter activity whereas in the DC area, where the other author is located, it is not as popular. That's not to say that lawyers in areas where Twitter is not popular shouldn't use it; but if you have a geographic-specific practice and your community is slow to adapt, you will probably want to bolster your social media presence through other tools in addition to Twitter.

Areas of Practice and Target Audiences
Some social media tools are more popular with certain audiences than others. Avvo, for example, generates substantial consumer traffic whereas LinkedIn is viewed by business and higher-income clients.

Ask yourself how will potential clients and colleagues be searching for you. Will they turn to Google? Will they seek referrals from colleagues and subsequently turn to the Internet to check your background and credentials? Will they search for you on the Web while sitting at their desk, or try to find a lawyer on the run using a mobile device?

Likewise, some segments of the population rely heavily on smart phones for Internet access. For example, a recent Pew Report study (**http://www .pewinternet.org/Reports/2009/12-Wireless-Internet-Use.aspx?r=1**) found that:

> *48% of African Americans have at one time used their mobile device to access the Internet for information, emailing, or instant-messaging, as compared to the national average of 32%.*

> *29% of African Americans use the Internet on their hand held on an average day, also about half again the national average of 19%.*

Thus, if you intend to target African Americans with your marketing, you'd do best by participating in social media sites that are easily accessed via mobile applications. As discussed in the last chapter, many more social media platforms are introducing mobile applications.

Personality and Preferences

The most important factors in choosing a suite of social media platforms are your personality and preferences—for two reasons. First, social media is about authenticity, and it's hard to be authentic if you're engaged in platforms that run against type. Second, a successful social media campaign requires consistency and you're more likely to stick to something that you enjoy.

Many lawyers are led to believe that blogging is the end-all and be-all of social marketing. Truth is, if you can't stand writing, blogging won't work for you; your posts will come across as tortured and, besides, they'll be erratic. If you want to create and circulate content about your field of expertise to show your familiarity but you don't enjoy writing regularly, then instead of maintaining a blog, you could write two or three short articles and post them on JD Supra, upload them to Facebook, or circulate the link on Twitter. Another shortcut to showcase expertise if you don't like writing is to serve as a resource: for example, you can gather court decisions and upload them to Docstoc and add limited commentary. You could include a link to the Docstoc compilation of documents as a resource for visitors to your website—who would also see that you're up to date on case law.

Ethics Considerations

Your state disciplinary authority may currently or eventually impose bar regulations that complicate your ability to participate in certain social media platforms. For example, a recent disciplinary ruling out of South Carolina (SC Bar, Ethics Opinion 09-10), see Part V and revised Florida Ethics Rule 4-7.2 (effective January 1, 2010) could make it difficult for lawyers licensed in these states to participate in Avvo. Other bars like Louisiana and New York had proposed rules that imposed additional and substantial costs on lawyers seeking to blog and could have deterred lawyers from blogging, though these rules were overturned as unconstitutional.[2] If your jurisdiction has restrictive rules governing certain platforms, you may be better off prioritizing those sites that are off the disciplinary committee's radar.

How can I learn more about the characteristics of a social media platform so that I can decide whether it's right for me?

You're in luck as resources on social media demographics abound. Much of the information on user statistics is available publicly at social media sites.

In addition, there are several websites and organizations that track and report on social media use. These include Nielsen Wire (**http://blog.nielsen.com/nielsenwire/category/online_mobile/**) and Pew Internet & American Life Project (**http://www.pewinternet .org/**), which regularly release reports on social media demographics and trends pieces. Econsultancy.com also offers numerous reports and whitepapers, with most summaries available at no cost (**http://econsultancy.com/reports**). Finally, in Appendix C, you'll find a Social Media affinity exercise that we've designed which will help you to select the platforms that are right for you.

---

[2] *See* Judge Declares Louisiana Advertising Rules Unconstitutional, *Lawyers Weekly USA* (August 4, 2008) online at **http://lawyersusaonline.com/blog/2009/08/04/la-rules-on-internet-ads-by-attorneys-are-unconstitutional/**, New York Ad Rules Found Unconstitutional, Niki Black, *Sui Generis New York Law Blog*, **http://nylawblog.typepad.com/suigeneris/ny_lawyer_advertising_rules/** (April 3, 2009).

CHAPTER SIX

Goal: Networking and Building Relationships

IN THIS CHAPTER, WE'LL discuss a goal near and dear to most lawyers' hearts and one for which social media is ideally suited: networking and building relationships. In the overview, we'll discuss the importance of transparency and authenticity in creating an online presence, and in the subsequent three sections, we'll discuss how to leverage your presence to accomplish the goal of networking and building relationships with other lawyers and potential clients.

Overview: The Importance of Personal Presence

Engaging in focused online participation and interaction is the best way to amplify and reap the benefits of your online presence. Of course, an individual's level of participation and interaction will vary from one platform to the next. The key to effective participation is to be genuine, transparent, and to provide useful and relevant information no matter what the context. Interact and converse, rather than merely broadcast and boast. Don't be afraid to occasionally share personal interests in addition to your professional ones. Doing so humanizes you and makes you appear more approachable to potential clients and other lawyers.

It is important to realize that social and professional networking necessarily overlap. Separating one's professional and social online identities and interactions is a mistake. It is the overlap between the two that makes a lawyer more likeable, more approachable, and more human.

> "Social media also provides a good opportunity for humanizing yourself. Generation Y is accustomed to using Google to learn more about you. Post/Tweet professional information and links, but if you also include tidbits that show you as a human being with interests outside the office it will make you seem more accessible."
>
> *—Ed Scanlon, Founder and CEO, Total Attorneys*

People would rather hire a lawyer with whom they can relate, connect, and understand. If you limit your social networking to a circle of people you already know, you miss out on the chance to interact with potential clients on a more personal level.

It is important to understand that successful networking doesn't occur in a delineated fashion. Lawyers who believe that they can or should control and separate their online networks are missing the point. In the process, they're also missing out on opportunities to connect with others, including potential referrers and clients.

> "Social media is not an activity that needs to be engaged in separate and apart from a larger objective. Once the lawyer knows what it is that he/she wants to accomplish, the next question should be—how can social media advance that goal? Social media is simply a communications channel that can be effective when utilized effectively and with intent. Without thinking about strategy and execution, value will be difficult to achieve."
>
> *—John Lipsey, Esq., Vice President,*
> *Corporate Counsel Services, LexisNexis*

An effective online presence revolves around visibility, relevancy, personality, and engagement. Find the forums with which you are most comfortable and put these principles to work.

It's not difficult to create an effective online presence for a law practice. Targeted social media interaction can be a very effective way for lawyers to network and promote their law practice. In the next few chapters, we'll show you how to accomplish this.

Social Media as a Tool for Networking with Colleagues

In most industries (law being no exception), personal referrals are the holy grail of a marketing strategy. Most likely, you've had far more luck converting leads into clients when a contact came by way of a trusted referral. It used to be that the only way to drum up referrals was through good old-fashioned legwork: attending networking events, lunching with clients, and participating in bar association activities. Though this kind of personal contact isn't necessarily costly, it can be time consuming. More-over, much of the interaction tends towards the superficial: after all, it's not as if you're going to dissect the Supreme Court's recent Fourth Amendment decision with a beer in hand at the bar or circulate your recent article on landlord tenant law at a baseball outing with colleagues.

Enter social media. Networking with your colleagues is one of the simplest goals that can be accomplished using social media. Online networking allows you to quickly and efficiently connect with fellow lawyers, both near and far. You can choose whether you would like to interact with colleagues in your geographical region, practice area, or even fellow alumnus.

One of the greatest benefits of online networking is the amount of flexibility that it offers you. Social media allows you to interact with other lawyers on your own terms and schedule. You decide where to focus your efforts and when to do so. You can determine what topics you want to discuss and those you'd prefer to avoid. Rather than networking at set times, such as during your lunch hour or after work, you can network at anytime, day or night.

There are a large variety of options available to you if one of your goals is to network with other lawyers. It's simply a matter of finding a few online platforms that work the best with your personality and with which you are most comfortable and that attract the types of lawyers whom you'd like to get to know better.

One way to connect with other lawyers is to locate and follow blogs in your practice area or your geographical region. It's up to you to decide where to focus your efforts. Depending on your areas of practice, you may find that regional blogs have the potential to result in more useful contacts than national blogs.

To initiate interaction, leave comments after posts that interest you. Engage in conversation in the comments with other readers and the owner(s) of the blog. If you have a blog or website, make sure that you leave a link when commenting, so that people will know who you are, while at the same time, allowing you to promote your practice and your blog.

If your law firm has a law blog, make sure to respond to people who comment on posts. Link to other law bloggers' posts, discuss the points raised, and offer your take on the issue. In other words, engage in a conversation with other bloggers. You'll make new connections, increase the number of incoming links to your blog—important for search engine optimization—and, perhaps, you might even learn something new.

You can also participate in online forums on lawyer-specific networks or join forums on more general online networks like LinkedIn and Facebook. Many of these forums are very active and a sense of community quickly develops between regular participants. For that reason, online forums are a great place to focus your efforts if one of your goals is to network with other lawyers.

Before jumping in and interacting on the lawyer-specific platforms, first ensure that you create a complete, robust profile by following the recommendations in Part IV. Then locate forums that interest you. Respond to posts and create your own. Get to know the other forum participants and participate regularly.

Reply to posts from other lawyers if you're able to offer useful commentary or information. Start new discussions relating to your areas of practice by asking for input regarding a change in the law, soliciting advice as to the procedures in a particular court or jurisdiction, or asking participants for opinions on how to handle a particularly thorny procedural issue. By participating in online legal forums, you'll gain useful information, increase your reach online, and network with new colleagues.

Another option is to network on Solosez, the ABA listserv, or other listservs, such as those sponsored by your local bar association. For those who are more comfortable interacting through email rather than online, listservs are a great alternative, even though they are not technically "social media." And, like online forums, you have the added convenience of connecting and interacting on your own schedule. Listservs can be a great resource, providing lawyers with information and support for their law practice. Local and regional listservs also offer the added benefit of allowing you to strengthen ties with other lawyers in your geographic area, and not just your own practice area.

> "I have been participating on email lists longer than on any other type of social media, primarily because the lists have been around longer than the newer tools (such as Facebook and Twitter). Law-related email lists are most useful, because they give me an opportunity to demonstrate my expertise to a focused audience (other solo and small firm lawyers)."
>
> —*Lisa Solomon, Esq., Legal Research & Writing, New York*

If you're comfortable with the medium, Twitter is another social media platform you may want to consider to achieve the goal of networking with other lawyers. Through Twitter you can connect with lawyers in your city (if you happen to live in a large metropolitan area) and with lawyers across the country. One advantage of Twitter is that there is no limit to the topics that you can discuss, whereas with forums, there is less of an opportunity to stray from the subject matter of the post to which you are replying.

On Twitter, you can discuss a large variety of topics, ranging from legal issues to personal hobbies and interests. This is because, as a networking platform, Twitter tends to be more informal than forums or blogs. Accordingly, many lawyers will occasionally discuss their personal interests in addition to their professional ones.

The informality of Twitter allows your personality to shine through and your professional colleagues may find themselves relating to you more easily because you share a common interest or hobby. You will find that a sense of camaraderie can develop very quickly through this medium, which helps facilitate your professional networking relationships.

It simply makes sense to expand your professional network using online platforms. It is a simple process that can be done on your schedule. It doesn't take much time to maintain the relationships and the benefits can be enormous. Your colleagues can act as a sounding board when you are faced with a perplexing legal issue. Your online professional network can also be a great information resource and serve as a regular source of referrals.

So, if you would like to expand your professional network, social media is a simple, time-efficient medium through which you can accomplish that particular goal. Choose the platforms with which you are most comfortable, dive in, interact, and watch your network grow.

Converting Online Relationships to Offline Relationships

Let's face it, while it's important to have a robust Internet presence and it's fun to pal around with friends and colleagues online on Facebook or Twitter, at the end of the day, an online relationship can go only so far. To truly maximize the power of social media, lawyers must, at some point, take their online relationships offline. The beauty of social media is that it allows you to meet and connect with people you would otherwise never have known. Social media amplifies your reach and breathes life into connections that have faded. Below are some tips and steps for taking the relationships formed online into the real world.

1. Whenever possible, meet your online connections in person. Transition your online connections offline. Strengthen the online contacts that you've made and use them to your benefit. For example, after connecting with local business people online, arrange to meet them for lunch. When traveling, meet online friends for coffee when visiting their hometown. Attend national legal conferences and network with the colleagues you've gotten to know through social media.

2. Use social media as an icebreaker at in-person activities. Social barriers come down quickly once you meet your online connections in person. After just a few minutes of conversation, you will likely feel as if you've known your online friend for years. An added side benefit to this phenomenon is that legal conferences can be both educational and entertaining.

3. Pick up the phone. Even if you don't anticipate meeting a colleague from social media in person anytime soon, there's no reason why you can't pick up the phone and call to introduce yourself. You'd be surprised at how adding a voice to an online image helps make it more robust.

4. Leverage online contacts into future business. If you've met someone online who you want to meet in person, use your online connection to set up an offline meeting.

Social Media as a Tool for Interacting with Clients

Network with Potential Clients, Promote Your Law Practice, and Increase Business

Maintaining an online identity, in one form or another, should be the crux of any law practice's marketing plan. People no longer reach for the

Yellow Pages when they need an lawyer. Instead, they ask friends for advice or seek information on the Internet. If your firm does not have an online presence that is easily located, you are undoubtedly losing potential clients left and right.

Some Social Media Advice

♦ "(Social media is) worthwhile for all (lawyers), but as in anything you need to do your homework and study/learn about each social media channel, what it does/what it can do, how others use it/suggest you use it."

—Gregory Bufithis, President, Posse Ranch, The E-Discovery Room

♦ "Worry more about being a good lawyer than (about) social media."

—Scott H. Greenfield, Esq., Criminal Defense Attorney, New York, New York

♦ "Social media is just another gathering place. You might prefer the country club, the golf course, or conventions. But if you don't ever open social media's door, you're going to miss the opportunity to be a founding member of the new country club, the improved world-wide convention, and the most readily available locker room at the virtual golf course. Why would you exclude yourself from that set of opportunities?"

—Victoria Pynchon, Esq., Mediator at ADR Services, Inc., California and arbitrator for the American Bar Association

♦ "The best value is realized from a consistent (online) presence, so the more an attorney can create and connect online, the better. I do qualify this: there is such a thing as overdoing and over-marketing and heartily caution anyone (from) engaging in this strategy to consider quality over quantity in their publishing and sharing."

—Martha Sperry, Esq., Associate Claims Counsel for OneBeacon Insurance Group; Principal, Advantage Advocates, Massachusetts

♦ "LinkedIn.com, by far, is the best social media platform for attorneys. Facebook appears to be useful for maintaining connections with friends and family. Twitter is an excellent source to broadcast particular issues in 140 characters or less. It is also a great way to publicize information about trends in your practice area and to develop an online reputation in a particular field."

—*Kenneth Suzan, Esq., Partner (IP, Internet Law), Hodgson Russ, LLP, Buffalo, New York*

♦ "The easiest networking platform to enter the social media party is Twitter. Yet in some ways it is the most complicated. As with any social media platform, if used for marketing your practice and networking with others, you have to know why you are there and the general rules of participation. With Twitter you need a URL in your biography so people can see who you are. If you haven't established your professional blog yet, then have a LinkedIn profile connected to your Twitter account so others can know who (you are)."

—*Susan Cartier Liebel, Esq., Founder, Solo Practice University*

♦ "Be nice. Be professional. Be yourself (unless you are mean and unprofessional). Don't post anything you wouldn't want the entire world to see. Use common sense. Be practical. When in doubt, look it up. Take 24-48 hours of cooling time before responding to something that makes you furious."

—*Rex Gradeless, lawyer in St. Louis*

Personal and Professional Networking Are Not Mutually Exclusive

Many lawyers fail to comprehend that separating one's professional and social online identities and interactions is a mistake. It is the overlap between the two that makes a lawyer more likeable, more approachable, and more human. A person's interests are not limited to their profession unless, of course, the person is an unbelievably one-dimensional and boring human being.

By way of example, one of the authors of this book regularly posts her dinner menu to Twitter, complete with links to recipes and photos of the end result. At one point, she conducted a poll to determine whether her followers, many of whom are lawyers, were put off by those decidedly nonlawyerly posts. As you can see, the results were overwhelmingly in favor of the tweets on that topic. (See Figure 6-1 below.)

In fact, when she is approached at local networking events and at legal conferences nationwide, the most frequent comment she hears is "I like your dinner tweets." There is a reason for that: quite simply, people are more than their careers. Social and professional arenas are not mutually exclusive. They can and should overlap—it is the overlap that makes all the difference.

Update Your Status and Interact on Social Networks

One of the simplest ways to interact online is to engage in conversations with potential clients using the status update feature on Facebook and LinkedIn. Use these platforms to engage with others, maintain professional and personal relationships and promote your practice and accomplishments.

Post your firm's most recent blog posts to your accounts on those sites, post occasional updates about your professional activities and accomplishments, link to interesting news stories relevant to your areas of practice, and comment on your connections' recent activities. By interacting and providing useful and relevant information, you are able to keep your law firm on your potential clients' and referrers' "radar."

Another way to connect with potential clients and referrers is through LinkedIn groups. First, join local and regional groups that are likely to have potential clients as members. Then, interact with other group members, and get to know them and learn about their business concerns. Finally, consider transitioning the online relationship to an offline one by suggesting a business lunch.

Figure 6-1. Results of a Twitter poll.

For example, if your law practice includes handling real estate matters, then joining a local LinkedIn realtors group would allow you to connect with and get to know real estate professionals in your area, who might then refer business to you.

Facebook also offers law firms a unique way to connect with potential clients: Facebook Pages (**http://www.facebook.com/advertising/?pages**). Facebook Pages is a relatively new concept that allows businesses to create a public profile on Facebook. Using your law firm's profile, you can then share your business with potential clients by connecting and engaging them.

As noted earlier, the utility of Facebook Pages for law firms has yet to be proven. Many law firms have created Facebook Pages, but their effectiveness is unknown since it is such a new tool. One of the difficulties with Facebook Pages is that you invite your friends to become "fans" of the page, a concept that works well for a band, for example. However, for a business that offers professional services, such as a law firm, the concept does not translate as well.

Will Your Clients Become Your "fans"?

"Every attorney should set up a Facebook fan page and encourage every single past and present client to join. You can advertise to draw new fans to your Facebook page, but how profitable that is remains to be seen. The clear payoff is in easily maintaining relationships with the people who can be your richest source of referrals."

—Ed Scanlon, Founder and CEO, Total Attorneys

That being said, given the large number of users and the huge amount of traffic that Facebook gets on a daily basis, many believe that Facebook Pages shows great promise for all types of businesses, including law firms. It may just be a matter of a few law firms thinking creatively and figuring out a way to use Facebook Pages to their benefit. Only time will tell how useful this tool will be for lawyers, but it's certainly unwise to write it off prematurely.

Connect and Engage on Twitter

Another social media platform to consider for engaging potential clients is Twitter. Twitter can be a useful social media platform for some lawyers seeking to increase their client base. For those with a national client base, Twitter is ideal. If your potential client base is local and you live in a large metropolitan area, Twitter also may work for you.

FACTOID #7

Ashton Kutcher and Ellen Degeneres (combined) have more Twitter followers than the population of Ireland, Norway, or Panama.[1]

The key to Twitter success—or success with any social media platform for that matter—is to set aside a small block of time each day to participate. When you do interact, be genuine, honest, kind, and generous.

Take off your lawyer hat. Don't be afraid to share your personal interests, such as sports, food and wine, or any other hobbies. As discussed above, doing so makes you more personable and approachable.

Follow our 50-30-10-10 rule. Fifty percent of "tweets" should provide followers with links to articles, blog posts, and other online content you think might be of interest; this percentage includes "re-tweets," or re-posts of tweets from other users, of relevant content. Thirty percent of tweets should be replies to other users' tweets—in other words, engage in conversations with others 30 percent of the time. Ten percent of tweets should consist of self-promotion, including your firm's blog posts and information about professional activities and accomplishments. Finally, tweet about your personal interests and hobbies about 10 percent of the time. Again, doing so will do much to humanize you, make you more interesting to your followers, and allow you to connect with nonlegal users who share similar interests.

Twitter Interaction Formula

- ♦ 50%—links to online content
- ♦ 30%—respond to and interact with others
- ♦ 10%—self-promotional tweets
- ♦ 10%—personal hobbies and interests

In summary, an effective online presence and the ability to generate new business because of your online interaction revolves around visibility, relevancy, personality, and engagement. Find the forums with which you are most comfortable (earlier, we made suggestions about factors to consider when selecting a social media platform to engage) and put these principles to work. Put in the effort and give it some time—it *will* pay off in the long run.

---

[1] http://socialnomics.net/2009/08/11/statistics-show-social-media-is-bigger-than-you-think/

A Contrarian View of Twitter

We're both fans of Twitter as a tool to build relationships with colleagues and clients. But not all agree. In May 2009, legal marketing expert Larry Bodine asserted on his blog that Twitter is not an effective law firm marketing tool. [SOURCE: **http://blog.larrybodine .com/2009/05/articles/tech/twitter-not-effective-for-law-firm-marketing/**] Bodine cited statistics showing that 60% of Twitter users leave after three months and that Twitter ranks as the least effective tool for boosting blog traffic compared with SEO, email promotions and blogs. Thus, Bodine concluded:

> After months of using Twitter, I've learned that it is a shouting post for relentless self-promoters, a dumping ground for press releases and advertising, an ego-driven competition to amass followers, and a target for computer-automated Tweets. It's always been a good place to learn what sandwich someone had for lunch and when someone changed a baby's diapers. But Twitter is supposed to be "all about the conversation," and I see few conversations that lead to new business.

Bodine's post spawned substantial debate throughout the blogosphere, with many Twitter fans jumping on board to defend the platform. *See e.g.*, **http://legalblogwatch.typepad.com/legal_ blog_watch/2009/06/more-reasons-to-use-twitter-not.html**. To be fair, at least Bodine gave Twitter a chance before reaching his conclusion. Many, however, do not, and instead write Twitter off based on perception and hearsay instead of testing it out for themselves. Because social media is such a personal tool, lawyers should try to sample a particular platform—including Twitter—instead of simply rejecting it reflexively.

Interestingly, just before this book went to the printer, Larry Bodine reversed his position and acknowledged the value of Twitter to lawyers (**http://www.lawmarketing.com/pages/articles.asp? Action=Article&ArticleCategoryID=58&ArticleID=1011**).

Twitter's a Toy

"Twitter is a total waste of time for anyone doing it other than to have some laughs with friends, become a social media guru or try to get business as a bottom feeder."

—*Scott Greenfield, criminal defense attorney, New York, NY*

CHAPTER SEVEN

Goal: Locate Information to Support Your Areas of Practice

ANOTHER WORTHWHILE GOAL that can be accomplished through social media is finding information online that will assist you in your day-to-day practice. There are a number of ways to use social media platforms to help you forward this goal. Using online tools, you can find summaries and analysis of the newest cases, laws, and trends that affect the areas of law that interest you. You can also be instantly notified when news breaks that may affect cases that you are handling by using Twitter, RSS feed readers, and Google news alerts.

Social media and online tools make it easy for you to stay on top of and manage information that will assist you with your law practice. It's simply a matter of locating the most helpful and useful sources, as explained below, and using online tools to bring the most relevant information directly to you.

RSS Feeds

The first step to locating relevant information is to sign up for an RSS feed reader. As we explain later in the book, Feedly (**www.feedly.com**) is our RSS reader of choice, but Google Reader (**www.google.com/reader**) and Bloglines (**www.bloglines.com**) are good choices as well.

Once you've created an account, the next step is to subscribe to law blogs that focus on the areas of law that you would keep up with. You can locate blogs of interest by searching for relevant terms at Google blog search (**www.blogsearch.google.com**) or reviewing the categories at a few of the larger law blog directories, such as Justia's blawg directory (**http://.blawgsearch.justia.com**) or US Law's directory (**http://www.us law.com/law_blogs**).

You can subscribe by clicking on the icons located in the sidebar of the blog, similar to those found on the right-hand side of the page below:

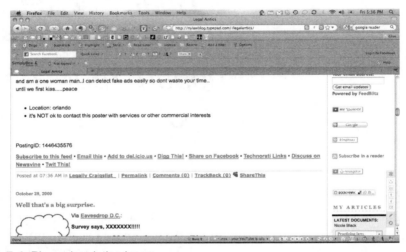

Figure 7-1. Blog subscription icons.

Once you've subscribed to the blogs that you would like to follow, new posts from those blogs will automatically appear in your RSS feed reader whenever you log into the reader.

For example, in Feedly, unread posts appear as follows:

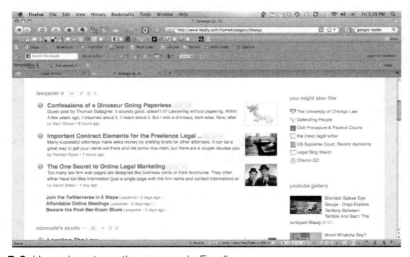

Figure 7-2. Unread posts as they appear in Feedly.

Once you click on a post and read it, the post will disappear from the Feedly page the next time that you log on.

In Bloglines, your feeds will appear as follows, with unread posts appearing in bolded print on the left-hand side of the page. Those posts that you have already clicked on and viewed will not be bolded, but rather will appear in regular print.

In other words, the names of blogs that have added new content which you have not yet read will be bolded. So, for example, in the screenshot below, the blog "Above the Law" has posted new blog posts and the title therefore appears bolded, whereas the blog below it, "All in the Family," has not posted new content so its name is not bolded. If you click on the blog "Above the Law," the unread posts will appear in the large frame to the right of the page and replace the text under the heading "web 2.0 lawyer—Google Blog Search" that currently fills that space.

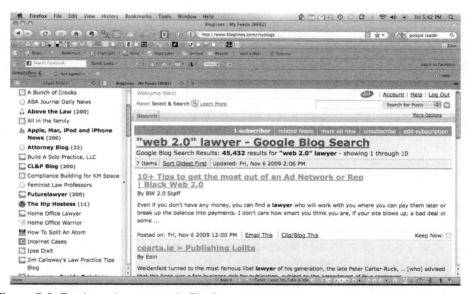

Figure 7-3. Feeds as they appear in Bloglines.

Another way to obtain information to support your practice is to subscribe to news searches for terms that are relevant to your practice. Once you create a Google news alert, Google will automatically search for news stories that contain the terms that you identify. You can then choose to receive emails when new stories appear or you can receive notifications of new stories in your RSS feed reader.

For instance, if you are an IP lawyer, you may choose to subscribe to a search for "patent law." To do this, you must first go to Google News (**http://news.google.com/**) and type in the search terms. At the very bottom of the page, click on the orange "RSS" button, as shown below.

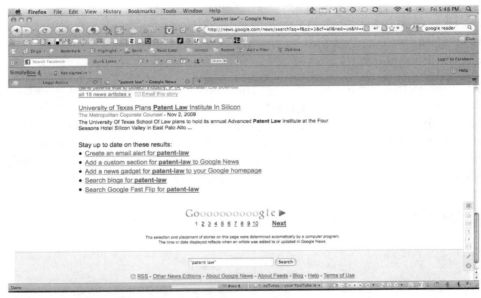

Figure 7-4. RSS button at bottom of Google News page.

Once you do so, you will be guided through the process of adding this news search to your RSS feed reader. After you have successfully subscribed to this search, all news items using those terms will automatically appear in your RSS feed reader.

After setting up a few carefully crafted searches, you will be on top of the latest news in your areas of practice. You'll know when groundbreaking cases are reported, analyzed, and discussed, offering you yet another way that your RSS feed reader can keep you on top of your game. In addition to keeping you up to date about the most recent news in your areas of practice, you'll also have information to share via social media. You can blog, tweet, and otherwise share the late-breaking news with your social media connections.

Twitter

Twitter is another really useful resource that can help you gain information to support your law practice. One way to accomplish this goal is to follow Twitter lists that have been curated by Twitter users. Some of these lists will include lawyers who practice law in your areas of practice. By following these lists, you will be able to track discussions between lawyers about some of the latest decisions that affect a given area of practice.

For example, if you practice criminal law, the "criminal law attorneys" list (**www.twitter.com/nikiblack/criminal-law-attorneys**), which was curated by one of the authors of this book, is good place to turn for the latest criminal law discussions, including links to recent blog posts and articles, all of which are posted by lawyers on Twitter who practice criminal law.

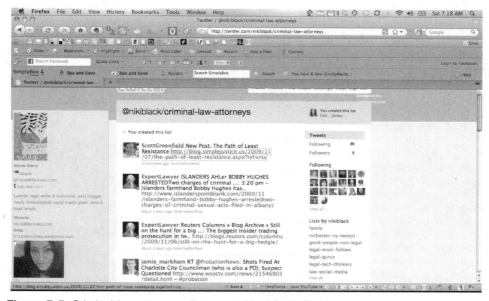

Figure 7-5. Criminal-law-attorneys list curated by Nicole Black.

Listorious (**www.listorious.com**) provides a directory of Twitter lists, making it easy for you to locate the lists that will help you stay on top of the areas of law that are most important to your practice.

Other useful online directories include Twellow (**www.twellow.com**), Just Tweet It (**www.justtweetit.com**), and We Follow (**www.wefollow.com**). These directories conveniently categorize Twitter users in a wide spectrum of areas, from aerospace and accounting, to small business and emerging market, to nonprofit, real estate, technology, and beyond. You can review the directories to seek out people with whom you'd like to connect based on their profession or interests.

In addition, there are two relatively new online directories of legal professionals on Twitter, both of which aggregate the Twitter streams of those included in the directories: Justia's LegalBirds (**www.legalbirds.com**) and LexBlog's LexTweet (**www.lextweet.com**).

Another way to find law-related conversations is via the Legal Tweets blog (**www.legaltweets.com**), which tracks legal topics currently being discussed on Twitter. The conversations are filtered to include trending issues and are edited to highlight the most salient points being discussed. (Disclosure: Legal Tweets is moderated by one of the authors of this book.)

As you can see, social media offers lawyers any number of benefits, not the least of which is helping you keep up with the latest news and changes in the areas of law that are the most important to your practice. If you utilize the right online tools, it's easy to quickly and efficiently locate relevant, timely information. It takes just a few minutes to set up these tools and the benefits will be more than worth the minimal up-front effort.

CHAPTER EIGHT

Goal: Gain Competitive Intelligence and Customer Feedback

LAWYERS CAN USE SOCIAL media for competitive intelligence about what others are doing and also to seek feedback from customers. We discuss these two related goals below.

Competitive Intelligence

A broad definition of **competitive intelligence** is the action of defining, gathering, analyzing, and distributing intelligence about products, customers, competitors, and any aspect of the environment needed to support executives and managers in making strategic decisions for an organization. [Source: **http://en.wikipedia.org/wiki/Competitive_intelligence**.] Locating competitive intelligence once required costly research by marketing companies, but these days, social media lets you do it yourself.

Realtime Search
Perhaps one of the most powerful tools social media offers for competitive intelligence purposes is realtime search. In July 2009, Wikipedia described the realtime Web as:

> [T]he concept of searching for and finding information online as it is produced. Advancements in Web search technology coupled with growing use of social media enable online activities to be queried as they

occur. A traditional Web search crawls and indexes Web pages periodically, returning results based on relevance to the search query. The real time Web delivers the most popular topics recently discussed or posted by users. The content is often "soft" in that it is based on the social Web—people's opinions, attitudes, thoughts and interests—as opposed to hard news or facts.

Now in its infancy, the realtime Web will soon be commonplace. It will allow instantaneous access to information on any topic or event as soon as that information becomes available, and as the event is occurring.

One tool that currently provides access to the realtime Web is Social Mention (**www.socialmention.com**). This is a great, free resource that allows you to conduct realtime searches of online social networking sites for mentions of you, your business, your competitors, and keywords that are relevant to your area of practice or other topics of interest to you. You can filter the search results to locate mentions from certain types of sites, such as Twitter, blogs, or video sites like YouTube. The search results also provide you with interesting data about the results, including whether the sentiment expressed in the results is positive or negative.

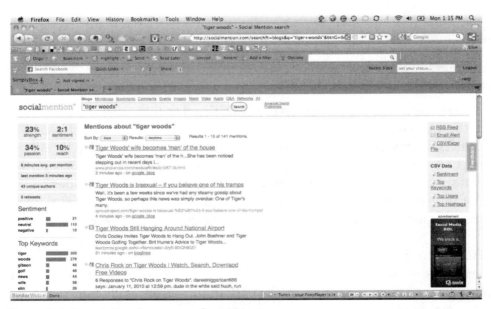

Figure 8-1. Search Results page on Social Mention.

By the time this book is published, you should be able to accomplish the same task using either Bing or Google's search engines. In October 2009,

Twitter announced agreements with Bing (Microsoft's search engine) and Google to allow both engines full access to its data, as produced in real-time. Microsoft also negotiated an agreement with Facebook that will allow Bing access to some of Facebook's data. These agreements take us one step closer to making the realtime Web a reality.

At first glance, that may not seem to be an earth-shattering concept, but it is a paradigm shift worthy of note. Lawyers should sit up and take notice. User-generated content, the fundamental building block of the "social Web," is now more influential. As a result of appearing in search engine results, as soon as it is created, it is instantaneously given more credence.

How does this affect the legal profession? The effects are countless. For example, criticism of legal employers appearing on Twitter has become infinitely more powerful. Negative comments regarding law school programs can be located in a heartbeat. And, tweets regarding trials in progress will become instantly searchable and available.

Small businesses, including law firms, that use Twitter or Facebook as part of their online marketing efforts can strategically tweak their marketing approach on those platforms to mirror trends and topics affecting their business, thereby appearing higher in search engine results.

Astute lawyers will use realtime search to locate issues and trends that may affect their areas of practice, and then tailor their marketing and litigation efforts accordingly. Class action attorneys, for instance, can search for realtime complaints about a particular drug or product and predict when or where a class of injured people may exist long before their technologically deficient colleagues get wind of it.

Make no mistake about it—realtime search finally is here, and it is going to alter the way that business is conducted.

Analytics

Many blog packages have a built-in "analytics" feature that will provide you with a variety of statistics about site traffic. Alternatively, you can install Google Analytics, a free tool that analyzes traffic to your site. In addition to showing the volume of traffic, an analytics tool will provide a variety of data, such as source of traffic (either direct hit, referral from another blog, or keyword search), visitor location, and the amount of time that visitors spend at your site. All of these statistics can yield useful information about the effectiveness of your social media activities.

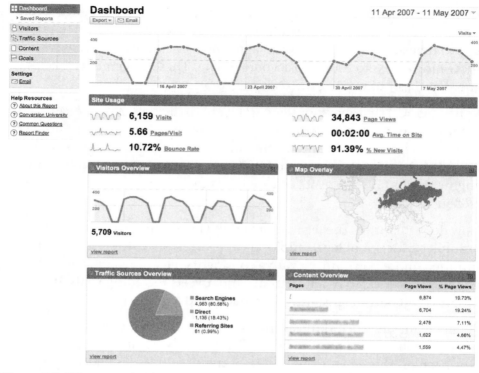

Figure 8-2. This screenshot is an example of the data provided by an analytics program.

Evaluating keyword searches that drive traffic to a blog may tip you off to promising practice areas. An increase in keywords like "lose my house," "foreclosure lawyer," or "mortgage scam" will tell you that there's a demand for information or legal assistance with foreclosure issues. Thus, you might decide to tweak your website to emphasize your foreclosure experience, or perhaps hold a seminar on foreclosure prevention that you could advertise on your blog or through Meetup.

Or, if you're an appellate lawyer blogging about cases in your jurisdiction, you might notice regular referrals to your blog from the court's website. This tells you that folks at the court—either law clerks, court staff or even judges—are reading your blog and presumably finding it valuable enough to return.

Finally, analytics can help you evaluate the effectiveness of a particular social media activity. For example, if you decide to circulate your blog posts to Twitter and your analytics data shows a significant rise in traffic in visitors referred by Twitter, then your participation in Twitter is helping you attract more readership, thereby increasing both the popularity of your blog (and enhancing your reputation), as well as your search engine visibility.

No longer does marketing online require a hefty budget and costly ad campaigns. With social media, you can inexpensively acquire information that lets you precisely target your marketing activities at trends or demands that emerge from analytics rather than taking a scattershot approach. And analytics also let you know whether certain social media activities are bringing you closer to your goals—or wasting your time.

Mining LinkedIn

For lawyers who represent businesses and companies, LinkedIn is a rich source of competitive intelligence on the industry. In *Harnessing Free-Flowing Competitive Intelligence Through Social Media Sites*, Greg Lambert and Steve Matthews describe how lawyers can use LinkedIn to gather information on a prospective client and industry trends:

> If the firm wants to bring in a company as a new client, one can easily look for that company under LinkedIn's "Companies" heading. From there, you can compile a number of pieces of information, such as how many employees have LinkedIn profiles. Based on those profiles, a good analyst can then build a list of the employees' names, titles, locations and the types of activities these employees perform for their company. New hires or recent promotions can be identified as well. LinkedIn also gives you an easy way to identify certain employees that are being mentioned in the news, referenced on blogs or active in LinkedIn's topic-area groups. Having information like this gives you an insider's scoop on some of the key players within the target company.
>
> Plus, by going to the "Related Companies" section of LinkedIn, one might unearth other trends within the company that could lead to a competitive advantage. In addition, identifying the top universities the executive staff attended, or what companies employees left to join this one, can help you better know the nature, quality and culture of the company you're targeting. LinkedIn's "Jobs" section can reveal if the company is currently hiring and may indicate if it is expanding in particular areas.[1] Note also, that as this book went to press, LinkedIn launched another feature, Company Follow (**http://blog.linkedin.com/2010/04/29/linkedin-company-follow/**), which allows users to keep track of key company developments.

---

[1] *ABA Law Practice Magazine* (Nov/Dec 2009) online at **http://www.abanet.org/lpm/magazine/articles/v35/is7/pg26.shtml**

Customer Feedback

One way that the nonlegal world designs and tweaks products and services is through customer input. For whatever reason, lawyers do not actively seek feedback from clients, which is a mistake. Even if you achieve a great result for your clients, nevertheless, they may be unhappy with matters that seem irrelevant to you—like a broken television in your reception room or your firm's practice of having a paralegal or junior associate provide status updates rather than the partner in charge of the case. As a result, they may not refer you to their friends, or if they do, they'll mention these deficiencies. Alternatively, clients may have high compliments for other policies, like your firm's client portal that lets clients access their own documents. Or they may admire some of the civic work that your firm supports, such as a charity soccer game or clothing drive at the school.

Through the interactive nature of social media, lawyers can learn from clients and consumers about the value of the service they provide, as well as their reputation in the community.

Ratings and reviews are an obvious source of client feedback. Some clients may provide unsolicited feedback on sites like Avvo, while with others you may need to be more proactive in eliciting comments. Ratings sites make it easier to automate the process of seeking client feedback (you can simply send a polite email with a link after closing out a file) and reduce some the awkwardness associated in asking for a testimonial.

Feedback is important for more than just client service—but can help your firm develop other activities to serve the community. For example, if your firm wants to raise money for a charitable cause, you could ask "fans" of your law firm's Facebook page about what causes they support and what kinds of fundraisers they prefer. After the event concludes, you can ask whether attendees enjoyed themselves and if they found the event worthwhile. Gathering feedback on your firm's civic activities will help you maximize the value of your contribution to the community.

CHAPTER NINE

Goal: Showcase
Your Expertise

"My blogging generates a lot of work for me, both directly and indirectly. I support the blogging with intense social networking via the above networks (LinkedIn, Avvo, INTA List, MH Connected, Cornell Lawyers Directory, JDSupra, Twitter), which raises my overall profile, establishes bona fides among colleagues and propels my traffic. It is not always clear what exactly is the source of an online-based client call, which I get several times a week—and I am loathe to interfere with the process of "closing" by asking too many questions which I have found the client or prospect can seldom answer all that usefully anyway."

—Ronald Coleman, Partner, Goetz Fitzpatrick LLP,
New York, New York

"Blogs have been my primary marketing tool. About 35-40% of my practice comes as a result of my blogs. For family law, blogs are the best marketing tool since they rank fairly high in Google search results. They also provide instant credibility with potential clients."

—Alexander Korotkin, Esq., Solo Practitioner
(Family Law, Bankruptcy, Criminal Law, Real Estate),
Rochester, New York

SOCIAL MEDIA IS THE ideal platform to expand your influence and showcase your expertise, effectively bringing your practice and your knowledge to the attention of colleagues, the media, and potential clients. If you use social media wisely and narrowly tailor your online activities toward the pursuit of specific goals, in this case, showcasing your expertise, you will easily stand out from the crowd.

The most effective way to achieve this is to create a strong online presence using the various platforms discussed in previous chapters. Once you've done so and have identified the online platforms with which you are most comfortable participating, the next step is to create and share your content, including blog posts, recent achievements, and media mentions.

Showcase Your Expertise, but Don't Forget to Interact, Too

Of course, keep in mind that sharing your content and achievements is simply one aspect of participating in social media. The key to effective online participation is to: (1) provide useful, relevant information, including your content and achievements, *and* (2) to interact, and converse with others. If you fail to engage with other users, you *will* fail at successfully using social media.

A variation of our 50-30-10-10 Twitter interaction rule discussed in Chapter 5 is equally applicable to how you spend your time online. Fifty percent of your online time should be spent providing followers with information that you think might be of interest; this time includes the time you spend drafting blog posts if you've chosen blogging as one of your social media platforms. Thirty percent of your online time should be spent engaging in conversations with others. Ten percent of your online time should consist of self-promotion on different social media platforms, including promoting your firm's blog posts and information about professional activities and accomplishments. Finally, if the social media platforms you have chosen to use allow for it, you should connect with other users by sharing your personal interests and hobbies approximately 10 percent of the time.

Social Media Interaction Formula

- 50%—provide followers with interesting content, including your blog posts
- 30%—Engage in conversation with others
- 10%—Self-promotion, including promoting your blog posts, professional accomplishments, etc.
- 10%—Sharing personal interests on appropriate social media platforms

Cross-Promote Your Content

One of the keys to achieving the goal of showcasing your expertise is to effectively cross-promote your online content. Make sure to use the tools available on different platforms to distribute and promote your content, thus bringing it to the attention of the people who matter the most to you. Doing so allows you to amplify and reap the benefits of your law firm's online presence.

> **FACTOID #8**
>
> More than 1.5 million pieces of content (Web links, news stories, blog posts, notes, photos, etc.) are shared on Facebook . . . daily.[1]

For example, Tweetdeck (**http://tweetdeck.com**) allows you to post to Twitter, LinkedIn, and Facebook simultaneously. Thus, with the single click of a button, you are able to instantaneously distribute information to your connections on all three platforms.

Another option is to use online tools to ensure that new blog posts are automatically posted to Facebook, Twitter, and LinkedIn. Some blogging platforms, such as Typepad (**www.typepad.com**) now allow you to do this through the blogging platform whenever you publish a new post.

If you have a Wordpress blog, which is a blog that uses Wordpress as its publishing platform, TwitMe (**http://wordpress.org/extend/plugins/twitme/**) is a Wordpress plugin that allows you to automatically publish blog posts to Twitter. WordBook (**http://wordpress.org/extend/plugins/wordbook/**) is a Wordpress plugin that allows you to post recent blog posts to Facebook.

Facebook makes it easy for you to import posts from one of your blogs directly to your Facebook wall as soon as you publish new content. Your Facebook wall is the timeline of activity that publishes to your profile and also appears in your friends' activity stream, thus sharing the information that you post to your profile with your Facebook friends. In order to do so, sign into your Facebook account, click on the "Applications" button in the bottom left corner, and then follow the instructions below, from Facebook's help center:

> **FACTOID #9**
>
> The fastest-growing segment on Facebook is 55- to 65-year-old females.[2]

---

[1] http://socialnomics.net/2009/08/11/statistics-show-social-media-is-bigger-than-you-think/
[2] http://socialnomics.net/2009/08/11/statistics-show-social-media-is-bigger-than-you-think/

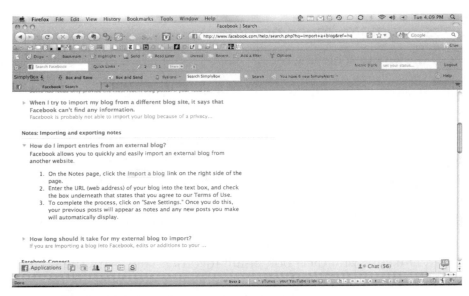

Figure 9-1. Facebook's help center.

Finally, another way to automatically publish blog posts to Twitter is to set up an account at Twitterfeed (**www.twitterfeed.com**). Once you have done so, it's a simple process to add the blog feeds that you would like to publicize on Twitter.

Do not overlook Twitter if one of your goals is to showcase your areas of expertise. Twitter is a great place to share content, expand your professional network, and obtain cutting-edge information relevant to a law practice or other areas of interest. Twitter has a very diverse user base and leaders in many professions are active on Twitter. Twitter makes it easy to interact with other lawyers worldwide, CEOs of major companies, innovators and thought leaders in all professions, as well as editors and journalists for major publications.

Syndicate Your Content Across the Web

You can also expand your online presence by distributing content and showcasing your work product by uploading documents to JDSupra.com. You can upload filings, decisions, articles, newsletters, blog entries, presentations, and media. Doing so allows you to capitalize on JD Supra's excellent SEO (search engine optimization) so that your work visibility will increase in search engine results when journalists or potential clients search for lawyers practicing in a certain area of law.

Once you've uploaded documents, JD Supra makes it easy to distribute the content to the profiles you've already set up on LinkedIn, Facebook, and Twitter. JD Supra has a full suite of online syndication tools that simplify the process, allowing you to quickly and easily distribute your content across the Web:

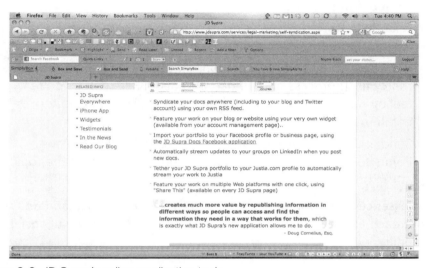

Figure 9-2. JD Supra's online syndication tools.

Social media is a fantastic, economical way to achieve any number of legitimate goals that will assist you in practicing law and promoting your law firm. A well thought-out plan of action will maximize the value of the time you spend online, making it worthwhile and beneficial for your law practice.

A Lesson in Repurposing Content: What Can You Do with a Month of Blog Posts?

Content counts when it comes to establishing expertise online. Here's one example of a strategy for repurposing blog content to get the most bang for the buck.

Let's say that over the course of a month, you write five blog posts describing the basic process for filing a Chapter 7 bankruptcy. Sure, you could leave those posts up at your site and do nothing more, but here are some ways to get more mileage:

- Run the feed for your posts through Facebook, LinkedIn, and Twitter so that your friends and followers can read them.
- Package the posts into a document—you can call it an e-book, an FAQ list, or even a whitepaper. Upload your e-book to sites like JD Supra or Docstoc.
- Take the knowledge you've gathered and prepare a Legal Guide for Avvo, to boost your presence on that site.
- Create a PowerPoint presentation/slideshow describing the bankruptcy filing process and upload it to SlideShare.net. If you're feeling particularly ambitious, you can also videotape your presentation and post it on YouTube.
- Send a copy of your e-book or link to your SlideShare Power-Points to several Meetup groups and offer to speak on the topic at the next meeting.

In essence, from one blog series, you can gain presence and do outreach at five additional platforms thanks to the power of social media.

Using Social Media to Attract Mainstream Media Attention

If you're looking for publicity for your practice, social media is a great way to find it. Many reporters regularly search blogs for commentary on current topics and will contact the blogger for questions. Likewise, reporters and news outlets participate in Twitter and occasionally reach out to those discussing a topic of interest or engaged in interesting activity.

Even if the press doesn't come to you, you can use social media to cultivate stronger ties to the press. Follow reporters and local news stations and try to help them out if they're ever looking for resources. If you sponsor an event—a webinar or meet-up through social media—invite reporters to attend and comp their admission. In many cases, they will graciously accept and even if they don't write a story, you'll have generated good will.

CHAPTER TEN

Goal: Branding Yourself or Your Law Practice

A brand is the set of expectations, memories, stories and relationships that, taken together, account for a consumer's decision to choose one product or service over another. If the consumer (whether it's a business, a buyer, a voter or a donor) doesn't pay a premium, make a selection or spread the word, then no brand value exists for that consumer.

—Seth Godin

LAWYERS HAVE BEEN SLOW to recognize the importance of branding themselves or their firm. Though we haven't found studies for the United States, a recent study out of the United Kingdom showed that more than 60 percent of the public could not name a single law firm, even though 78 percent had used a solicitor before.[1] But if clients can't remember or identify your firm (especially if they've used it once before), they can't hire you or refer you to others. Likewise, without a brand, other lawyers or colleagues won't recall what sets you or your firm apart and will have no reason to refer you over your competitor to a prospect.

A brand is much more than a stylish logo. As Seth Godin explains, a brand—more specifically you or your firm's brand—is a set of memories, stories, and relationships that motivate a consumer to choose you over a competitor. In short, a brand is more than what you do; it is, in essence, who you are. Because social media is all about building relationships and exchanging stories, it's an ideal tool with which to establish a brand.

---

[1]http://www.lawgazette.co.uk/news/public-unable-name-a-single-law-firm-research-shows

Social media gives you tools to establish a brand—the brand of you. One lawyer who has effectively used social media to brand himself as the go-to "foodborne illness outbreak" lawyer is Seattle, Washington, based Bill Marler. Through his prolific and popular blog and Twitter feed, Marler

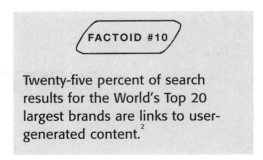

Twenty-five percent of search results for the World's Top 20 largest brands are links to user-generated content.[2]

churns out a stream of information on outbreaks of foodborne illnesses.

Figure 10-1. This screenshot shows The Marler Blog on food poisoning outbreaks and litigation.

But Marler's brand is about more than disseminating information on foodborne viruses. After all, an RSS feed or news service could do that. Rather, Marler takes social media a step farther: Marler's blog shares stories of some of the heartbreaking cases he's witnessed in his years of practice, and describes his ongoing efforts to secure regulatory reform and new laws to proactively address the problem of foodborne illness. Marler isn't just knowledgeable like so many other lawyers, but his social media activities show that he is compassionate and committed as well. That's Marler's brand as a lawyer and what helps distinguish him from others in his field.

---

[2]http://socialnomics.net/2009/08/11/statistics-show-social-media-is-bigger-than-you-think

Figure 10-2. Marler's Twitter stream provides updates on recent e-coli outbreaks.

A brand not only sets you apart from the competition, it makes you memorable. Gerry Oginski, a New York medical malpractice lawyer, uses video and YouTube to brand himself as a hands-on, hard-working lawyer who recognizes the power of video. Oginski has created several hundred videos, available on YouTube, that discuss cases that he's handled, explain legal issues, and offer testimonials from clients. Watching the videos gives viewers a sense of the kinds of cases that Oginski handles (they range from major suits to smaller yet compelling matters), how he does business (he's not a volume practice or mill) and most of all, his enthusiasm and dedication for the law and his clients. You can't cultivate that kind of branding in a 30-second television commercial.

CHAPTER ELEVEN

Goal: Increasing SEO and Improving the Quality of Leads

SEO STANDS FOR "search engine optimization." SEO refers to various practices—from buying paid links to strategic use of search terms within posts—that increase the visibility of a site on Google and other search engines. In short, SEO focuses on getting you to the first page of Google, preferably in the top three results.

There used to be a time that SEO was a numbers game. Improve traffic to a website and increase its ranking on Google. But investing in SEO can be costly, not to mention dangerous, with companies engaging in activities that could actually penalize your website in Google's search engine.[1]

As discussed below, social media has the effect of increasing lawyers' SEO. In fact, that's why social media appeals to so many marketers and so-called SEO experts. Although for the sake of completeness, we offer some tips on how to leverage social media to improve SEO, we strongly believe that using social media just to boost page rankings squanders social media's awesome power. You're far better off engaging social media to

---

[1] For example, in 2008, Findlaw was using paid links to game Google and earn better search engine placement for customers who paid dearly for Findlaw listings. When Google discovered the activity, it temporarily downgraded Findlaw's page rank, thereby reducing the search engine visibility for firms that had signed up for Findlaw's program. *See* Elefant, Legal Blogwatch (September 5, 2009), online at **http://legalblogwatch.typepad.com/legal_blog_watch/2008/09/finding-out-mor.html**

produce and disseminate great content, to educate clients and the public, and to participate in meaningful discourse and light-hearted banter with other lawyers and colleagues. After all, though SEO may lead clients to your site, if it's devoid of content, testimonials (if ethically permitted), and any semblance of personality, why would site visitors want to hire you anyway?

Search Engine Optimization (SEO)

Hands down, the best way to improve your online SEO is to produce high-quality content and disseminate it in a manner that increases its online visibility. Some suggestions follow.

Content

You can produce content either by writing posts at your blog or posting documents on JD Supra or the other archiving sites. At your blog, strive for commentary that's interesting, timely, comprehensive, or controversial because that will increase the likelihood that other bloggers will link to your posts. Incidentally, the value of an "organic link" (a link within a post) carries far more value on Google than having your blog linked in the sidebar of another blog. In addition, link to and discuss posts by other bloggers. When you start a conversation in the blogosphere, others will join, which will also bring additional traffic to your site.

Tagging and Headlines

Tag your content (e.g., blog posts or uploads to Docstoc) to make it easier to track. For instance, if you upload a set of recent employment law cases to Docstoc and tag them as "employment law" or "employment discrimination," the uploads will attract users searching Google for those topics to your site. Employ tagging at your blog, but also use powerful, descriptive content, since that's what gets picked up by Google. For example you write an analysis on a pivotal Texas appellate case in Smith v. Jones that involves the Fourth Amendment. Don't title your post "A summary of today's ruling" or "Smith v. Jones: a Summary." Instead, try something like, "Texas Court of Appeals says no Fourth Amendment protection for state employee texting on the job in Smith v. Jones."

Comments

Most bloggers welcome comments because they're where the conversation happens. Some blogs, like Dan Harris's "China Blog" receive dozens of substantive comments on a daily basis, thus further reinforcing the popularity of his blog. In fact, comments are often the most interesting part of a blog, and thus make the blog more appealing to other readers.

So comment freely on other blogs to further the conversation. In fact, by doing so, you may enjoy a residual boost in SEO if the comment section contains a link back to your blog.

However, there's one important caveat. Do not post generic comments on popular blogs (e.g., "Nice post" or "Good work") for the purpose of getting a link back to your site and enhancing SEO. Many popular bloggers, like Scott Greenfield of Simplejustice.us, Mark Bennett of Defending People (**www.bennettandbennett.com/blog**), and Eric Turkewitz (**www.newyorkpersonalinjuryattorneyblog.com**) have caught on to the practice of "comment spam" (i.e., posting generic comments, like "Great post!" or "Nice job!") to game SEO—and they are "outing" the offenders by name in posts at their sites. Bear in mind that it's not enough to refrain from comment spam yourself. If you retain an SEO or marketing expert, you are responsible for making sure that they don't post worthless comments at blogs on your behalf.

Capitalizing on the popularity that other bloggers worked to build through comment spam just isn't right. Moreover, these kinds of sleazy tactics run counter to one of the underlying purposes of social media, which is to deepen, not cheapen, relationships.

Quality of Leads

Not only does social media help with SEO, but more importantly, it can improve the quality of leads that you receive. Thus, instead of getting 30 calls a month from your website through conventional SEO with only two calls converting into clients, social media may cut the number of calls to 20 (by helping to eliminate unsuitable clients), while increasing the conversion rate to five calls.

How can social media improve the quality of leads? It can do so in three ways. First, tools like blogs and e-books uploaded to JD Supra, or video, can educate clients about the types of cases that you handle and describe the elements of a worthwhile case. For example, a blog post entitled "Why You May Be Earning Too Much Money to File for Bankruptcy" may screen out callers who don't qualify. Second, blogs and fan pages help educate referral sources, like friends and colleagues, about what you do. Consequently, they'll stop sending you completely irrelevant cases that you don't have the expertise to handle and, instead, will prescreen potential referrals to ensure that their legal matters are within the scope of your practice. Third, by reviewing analytics data from blogs (see discussion on page 101), you can learn what keyword search terms are bringing clients to your site. Let's say that you review the analytics and discover that the majority of your blog visitors are interested in elder care issues, which also happens to be your favorite practice area. By bulking up your blog with more posts on elder care, you can target your marketing efforts to reach precisely the segment of clients whom you want to represent.

PART FOUR

The Nuts and Bolts of Setting Up Social Media Profiles and Engaging in Social Media

CHAPTER TWELVE

Getting Set Up

THIS SECTION WILL DISCUSS some of the basics associated with getting set up on a social networking site. Even though there are a variety of sites, most of the registration features are common to all, as we will discuss.

This chapter is organized as follows: In the first section of this chapter, we'll summarize the general rules for registration and creating profiles common to all sites. In the second section, we'll post screenshots to walk you through the registration and profile creation for LinkedIn and Facebook.

General Rules for Registration and Creating Profiles

Registration

All social networking sites will require you to register and enter user information. We strongly recommend that you use your name (or your law firm's name) as a username for the sites for which you register. Disclosing your identity at the outset promotes authenticity and transparency, both of which are imperative for a successful social media experience. For the sake of convenience, choose the same password for all your social media sites. However, take appropriate security measures when selecting a password (e.g., don't use "password") as there have been situations where hackers have managed to hack into profiles.

Be sure the email that you use to register at the site is one that you check frequently. That way, when there's an update to your site or a request to connect, you'll receive an email notification. As discussed below, the most efficient way to keep abreast of changes at a social media platform is via email alerts rather than daily site visits—and if you don't regularly check the email that you use to register, you'll miss out on those updates.

Free versus Paid?

With any social media platform, opt for the free service at the outset. In fact, the free version of every platform we've discussed (with the exception of blogs) is fully functional for most lawyers' social media purposes.

Photos

Most sites offer the option of including a photo, which we strongly recommend. First, a photo gives your profile a personal touch and shows that you took added care to develop a complete profile. A photo also serves a practical purpose; it lets people whom you've met offline identify you if you ever meet in person.

It's not necessary to use the same photo for all platforms. Instead, match the form of the photo to the function of the site. In other words, use a professional quality photo for sites like LinkedIn or Avvo, preferably some kind of portrait headshot (though there are high-end options, you can arrange for fairly inexpensive digital headshots from stores like Sears, JC Penney, or Target). For more socially oriented sites (or sites that you use for more social purposes), use a casual photo that conveys the relaxed or friendly side of your personality. Obviously, even your casual photos should be in good taste; needless to say, avoid shots where you're inebriated, scantily dressed, or posed in a provocative manner.

Review the Terms of Service (TOS)

Every social media platform contains terms of service, which are basically the rules by which one must abide in order to use the service. Usually, such terms are legally binding. [Source: **http://en.wikipedia.org/wiki/Terms_of_service**.] TOS will generally describe how a site may use information, where it is stored, how it is disseminated, and what types of contact will give rise to a violation that could get you kicked off the site. A few months back, Facebook raised some controversy when it changed its terms of service to allow it to claim ownership of users' photos, wall posts, and other content—even after users had closed their Facebook accounts. Users rebelled and Facebook withdrew the proposal.[1] Given that lawyers use social media platforms for professional reasons, it's important for lawyers to understand the TOS to ensure that a social media site won't use

---

[1] *See* PopCrunch.com (February 18, 2009), online at **http://www.popcrunch.com/facebook-terms-of-service-controversy/**

their profiles or content in an undignified manner or in a way that could result in a violation of applicable ethics rules. Finally, you should monitor changes to a site's TOS and policies as the site evolves. A recent post at the Electronic Freedom Foundation's (EFF) blog shows how privacy policies have changed (and in EFF's view, been eroded) as the site has grown. See **http://www.eff.org/deeplinks/2010/04/facebook-timeline**.

Privacy Settings

As mentioned earlier, some social media platforms like Facebook or Twitter support both professional and personal interaction. Though most lawyers have enough discretion to avoid posting lewd or compromising photos of themselves, you can't prevent friends from posting those old fraternity pictures and tagging a picture of you wearing a lampshade.

Fortunately, Facebook offers several privacy options. Users can make their entire Facebook page publicly visible to all Facebook users, or they can limit access to their friends. You can also refine your privacy settings further, to allow only certain friends to view photos or read your wall posts. By using Facebook's privacy settings, you can friend clients and professional contacts knowing that they won't be privy to the more embarrassing moments of your life. At the end of this chapter, you'll see the screenshots of how to set privacy settings.

Like Facebook, Twitter also offers certain privacy options. You can keep your tweets private or block other users from following you.

Rules for Creating a Profile

Take the time to complete the full profile

There's nothing worse than a barren, partially filled profile. If you go to the trouble to activate your profile, take the time to fill it out as comprehensively as possible. For some sites like Twitter, completing a profile is a quick exercise—after all, there's not much to say in 140 characters. Other sites, like LinkedIn or Avvo, will require more work because you'll want to list your full history including schools, employment and education, past publications, and the like.

Use keywords in creating your profile to attract your target audiences

Keywords are basically those words or phrases associated with you or the services that you provide and that users are most likely to employ to search for a similar service online. For example, a family law attorney in

Texas might select "Texas family law attorney" or "family lawyer in Texas" as a descriptive keyword phrase to include in an online profile. Or a lawyer who uploads a sample nondisclosure agreement to JD Supra might tag the document with his name, the name of his law firm, and descriptive terms like "California NDA."

The tagging features on heavily trafficked sites, like Docstoc or LinkedIn, are super-charged, and strategic use of keywords can catapult your profile or document (which in turn will link to your profile or website) to the first page of a Google search results.

Tag word and keyword selection is a topic unto itself, but here are a couple of tips to get started:

♦ Google tools like Google Adwords or Google Trends can give you an idea of the terms that users search on a daily basis.

♦ Run some searches yourself using certain search terms and see where your existing website ranks compared to the competition. Review competitors' sites to get a sense of the words and phrases that they use to generate their positioning.

♦ Use geographic locations in your keyword phrases if you have a regional or local practice. Finding people on a local level can be difficult and using "locational" terms (e.g., Buffalo, New York) in your keywords can help you stand out.

♦ Educate yourself on SEO through sources like **www.seobook.com** or from Google itself with its SEO Starter Guide, **http://google webmastercentral.blogspot.com/2008/11/googles-seo-starter-guide.html**.

Use powerful active words and phrases to create your profile

With so many profiles online, it's important to create one in a way that captivates users. Don't settle for a bland, passive voice, but instead use powerful active words and phrases. Review other profiles for ideas.

Use your profile as an opportunity to share your story. Employ a narrative and try to personalize your experience. Even though profiles offer a standard, cookie-cutter form, you can still make them sing with vibrant language that conveys your philosophy and your personal story.

Proof your profile

As with any lawyer communication, you should carefully proofread your profile. An error-ridden profile suggests that you're careless or not detail prone, which isn't the sort of image that a lawyer wants to convey.

Claim the "short URL" for your profile

Most social media sites offer a "short" URL form (e.g., **www.facebook.com/carolynelefant**) for your profile. Claim the short profile so that it's easier to display in the signature line of your email or on business cards.

Take advantage of tools that let you track changes at the site

When you sign up for most social media sites, you'll be asked whether you want to receive updates by email. Receiving notice of an update by email is far more efficient than visiting the site on a daily basis to monitor it.

Take advantage of convergence tools

Some social media sites, like LinkedIn or Facebook, will let you import feeds from blog posts or Twitter. Take advantage of these tools because they provide an easy way to redistribute content to a broader audience. (*See* screenshots for set-up.)

Invite connections

Once you've registered for a site, you can friend (Facebook), follow (Twitter), or link with (LinkedIn) other users. Start with your own contacts. Most of the sites make it easy for you to select an option that will search your email to determine whether current contacts are already using a particular platform. After you've mined your contacts, use the search features at the social media sites to hunt around for other interesting folks whom you'd like to connect with. On sites like LinkedIn, take a look at your existing colleagues' contacts, and if there's someone on their list who you'd like to meet, request an introduction.

Abide by "net-iquette" rules when seeking connections

If possible, include a brief personal note in a request to connect. These days, lawyers are inundated with requests to connect and to friend colleagues, so including a brief note in your request is a welcome courtesy. And of course, you should explain how you know the potential connection (or why you want to get to know her) if you anticipate that they won't recognize you. Below are two examples:

> **Example 1:** Dear Joe, Hi, we've exchanged emails on the XYZ listserve for two years now, so I thought it might be worthwhile to connect up on LinkedIn. Best, Jane

> **Example 2:** Dear Ms. Jones, [don't use first names unless you have an existing relationship] I'd like to introduce myself—I'm an alum of New York law school and I'm very interested in the work that you're doing related to green buildings and energy efficiency. In fact, I'm a loyal reader of your blog. I handle energy efficiency matters in Texas and I'd

like to connect in the hopes of eventually exploring ways we might work together. Sincerely, Richard Roe.

Other net-iquette tips include:

+ Don't link to people you don't know.

+ Don't ask people to connect just for the sake of gathering links—it's annoying.

+ Don't send blanket emails to large listserves asking to connect. Listserve participants spend enough time sorting through mail from the listserv.

Seek recommendations and testimonials

Once you've registered and invited connections, seek testimonials and recommendations from close colleagues, past co-workers, and clients (though bear in mind any ethics restrictions that might apply). In particular, avoid asking for a reciprocal recommendation—e.g., "If you endorse me, I'll endorse you." Giving something of value for a positive recommendation raises ethics red flags. (See Part V—The Ethical and Legal Issues of Social Media.)

Testimonials and recommendations help personalize your profile and let others know about your special talents from a source other than you.

Getting Testimonials From Clients

The best testimonials from clients are spontaneous—the ones that appear on your LinkedIn profile or Avvo without you ever having had to ask. However, in many cases, clients are not familiar with sites like Avvo or LinkedIn and, therefore, won't post a testimonial unless you request it.

Asking for a testimonial can be tough, even when you've done a great job, because it may feel as if you're fishing for compliments. Still, the ability to reference sites like Avvo or LinkedIn can make the request process less awkward. For example, when you send a letter or email to a client closing out a matter, you might add:

> My firm is listed on (Avvo or LinkedIn) and it would be very helpful to me if you could take the time to complete this online client rating process—[insert link to ratings page]

By the way, don't ask for client testimonials while a case is pending. Some jurisdictions, like New York, don't allow it and you never know how the case will turn out.

Profile Creation

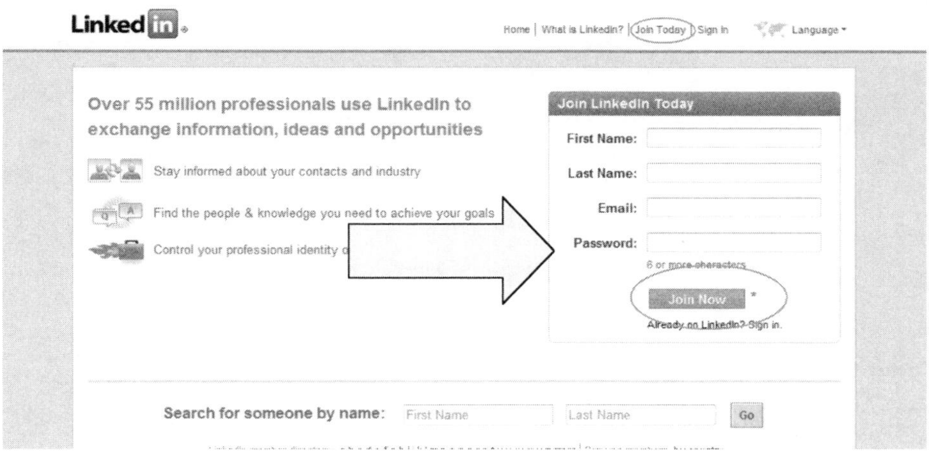

Figure 13-1. LinkedIn's registration page.

Step 1: The screenshot shows LinkedIn.com. This is the page where users register for LinkedIn and where they can sign in once they've registered.

To register for LinkedIn, click on the "join now" button. After you've completed the registration form, you'll receive an email asking you to confirm your registration.

Once you've confirmed your registration, return to LinkedIn.com, only this time, click the "sign in" button on the menu bar at the top of the page. After you've done that, the sign-in page below will appear.

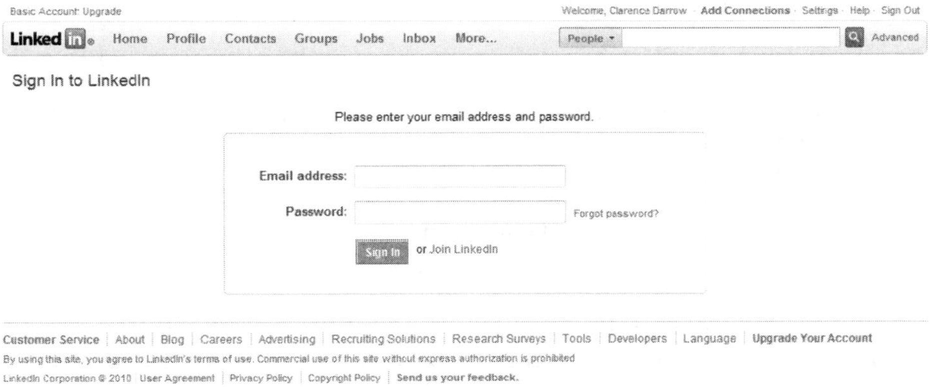

Figure 13-2. LinkedIn's sign in page.

Once you sign in, the screen below will appear, which will help you identify users whom you may already know on LinkedIn.

Figure 13-3. Identifying users on LinkedIn.

To find users you already know, select the mail program that you use. LinkedIn will automatically pull up your email contacts and identify those on LinkedIn.

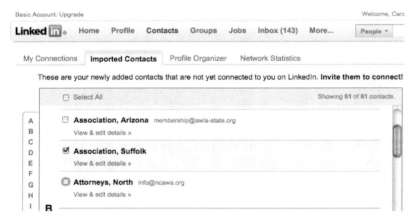

Figure 13-4. This screenshot shows the email contacts that LinkedIn retrieved from a user's email account. Users can designate which of the contacts they want to send an invitation to connect by checking the box next to the contact's name.

You can choose whom you'd like to invite from the contacts retrieved by LinkedIn by checking the box next to their name.

Though it's preferable to personalize connection requests on LinkedIn, when you're getting started, it can be onerous to send individualized invitations. So take advantage of LinkedIn's auto-invite tool, at least for those contacts with whom you already have a fairly close working or personal relationship.

After you've selected your contacts, click on the "profile" button in the menu bar (see menu bar on the screenshot above) and select "edit profile" from the drop-down menu.

Figure 13-5. This screenshot shows the view that you'll see when you select "edit profile." The screenshot shows where you can add information on current and past positions, ask for recommendations, and add a link to your website and Twitter feed.

Enter Information

Once you've selected "edit profile," you can start entering information on your current employment position, past employment, and education.

LinkedIn allows you to enter more than one current employment position, so if you're working at a firm but also teach as an adjunct professor at the local law school, you can list both positions as current.

Customized URL

In the last line of the profile information, you have the option of creating a customized URL for your LinkedIn profile (e.g., **www.linkedin.com/johnsmith**). Take advantage of this feature to make it easier to put your LinkedIn URL on business cards or in the signature line of your email.

Summary and Specialties

In addition to inputting information about current and past employment, complete the "Summary" (which is located underneath the profile information). The Summary will appear right under your name in your profile and serves as an encapsulation of all of your professional competencies. Underneath your Summary, you have the option of listing "specializations." As discussed in Part V on Ethics, some lawyers believe that listing a specialization may violate the rule in many jurisdictions preventing lawyers from holding themselves out as specialists. Thus, they include a disclaimer to the effect that "The Florida Bar doesn't allow lawyers to claim 'specialties' but I focus my practice on. . ."

Profile Creation: Facebook

Figure 13-6. Facebook's sign-up page.

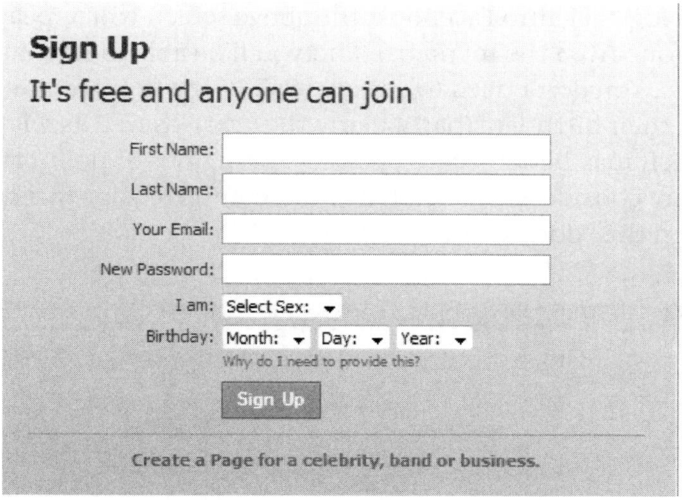

Figure 13-7. Page view for Facebook registration.

The sign-up process for Facebook is very similar to LinkedIn. When you go to Facebook.com, you'll see a sign-up form. Once you fill it out, you'll receive an email notification, which you must retrieve to activate your Facebook account.

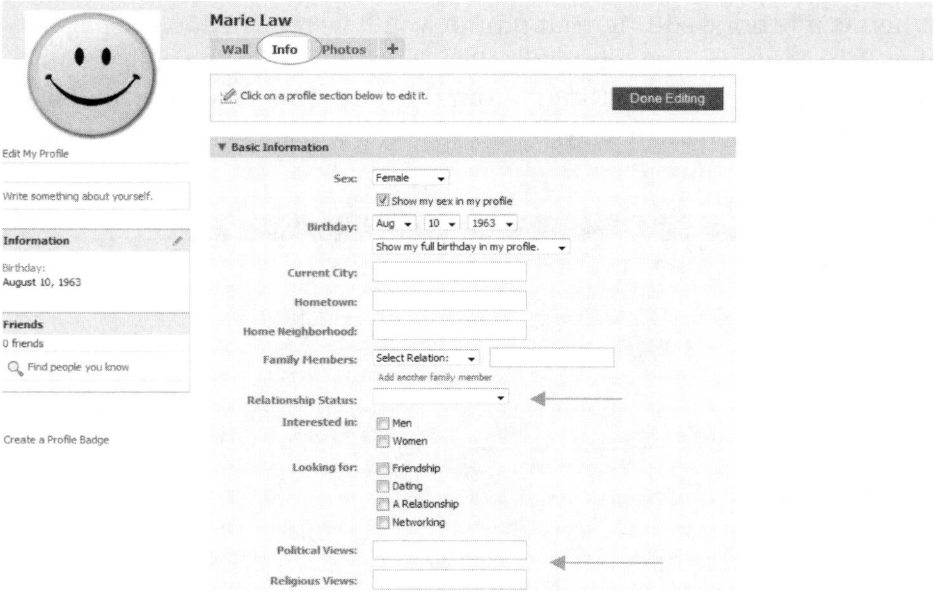

Figure 13-8. Sample Facebook account page.

When you log back into Facebook, the above screen will appear. Select "information" from the menu bar, and you'll be able to start filling in your profile. You don't need to complete all of the fields requested. Many users omit their birthdate (particularly the year), as well as relationship status, which may be subject to change, or religious or political views, which many consider personal. Once you complete your Facebook profile, click on the "done editing button."

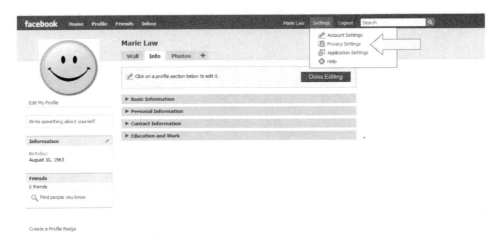

Figure 13-9. Facebook screenshot with privacy settings.

When you're done editing your profile, you'll be returned to the page above. To access privacy options, select "settings" from the blue menu bar, and select "privacy settings" from the drop-down menu, which will take you to the screen displayed in the next screenshot.

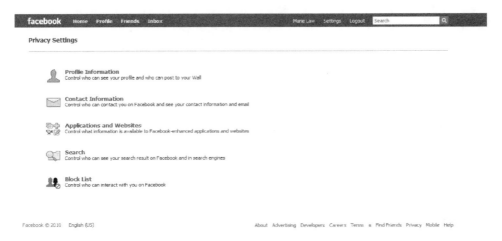

Figure 13-10. Privacy settings screenshot.

The screen on the previous page describes all of your options for privacy settings. You can control those portions of your profile that you want visible, limit access to contact information, and block other users from interacting with you.

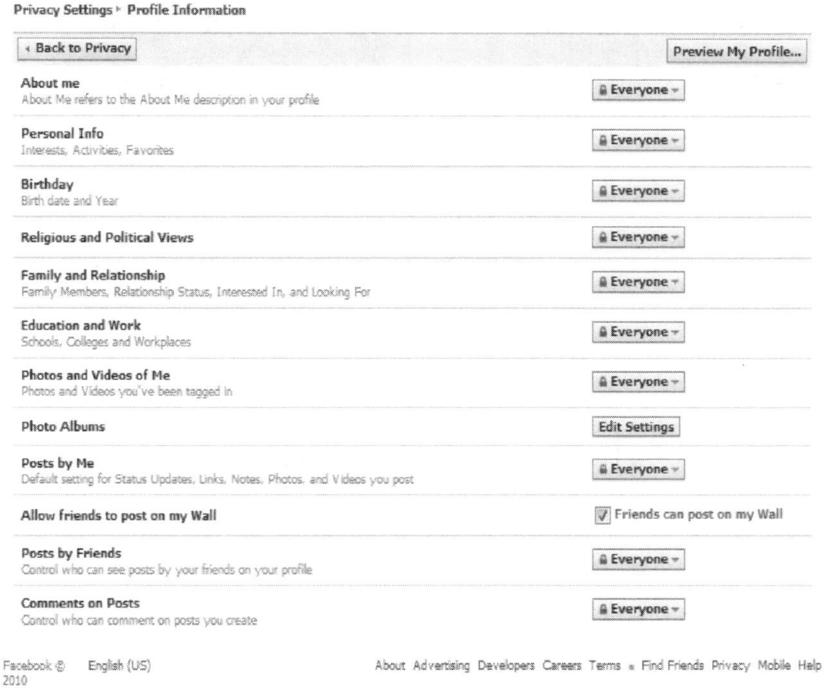

Figure 13-11. This screenshot shows privacy setting options for a profile page. This user has made all aspects of her profile public, i.e., viewable by "everyone."

Figure 13-12. View of button for "custom privacy settings."

The buttons on the right offer a drop-down menu that you can use to set privacy settings on "everyone" (public) or (private). There's another option as well—you can customize settings by selecting "Customize" from the drop-down menu on the buttons at right. After hitting "customize settings," you'll have access to the box in the center of this page, which allows you to make information visible only to specific people.

Facebook also lets you control the privacy settings on photos and videos where you're tagged. To block access to tagged photos, select "Photos and Videos of Me" from the menu on the left.

Figure 13-13. Facebook options for blocking access to tagged photos.

Then, by clicking on the button on the right, choose "customize"—and you can specify which users (if any) may have access to tagged photos.

Privacy Settings ▸ Profile Information

◂ Back to Privacy	Preview My Profile...
About me About Me refers to the About Me description in your profile	🔒 Only Friends ▾
Personal Info Interests, Activities, Favorites	🔒 Only Friends ▾
Birthday Birth date and Year	🔒 Only Friends ▾
Religious and Political Views	🔒 Only Friends ▾
Family and Relationship Family Members, Relationship Status, Interested In, and Looking For	🔒 Only Friends ▾
Education and Work Schools, Colleges and Workplaces	🔒 Only Friends ▾
Photos and Videos of Me Photos and Videos you've been tagged in	🔒 Only Friends ▾
Photo Albums	Edit Settings
Posts by Me Default setting for Status Updates, Links, Notes, Photos, and Videos you post	🔒 Only Friends ▾
Allow friends to post on my Wall	☐ Friends can post on my Wall
Comments on Posts Control who can comment on posts you create	🔒 Only Friends ▾

Figure 13-14. Facebook privacy settings options.

You can repeat the same steps to protect any aspect of your Facebook information. The screenshot above shows where you can block users from posting on your wall.

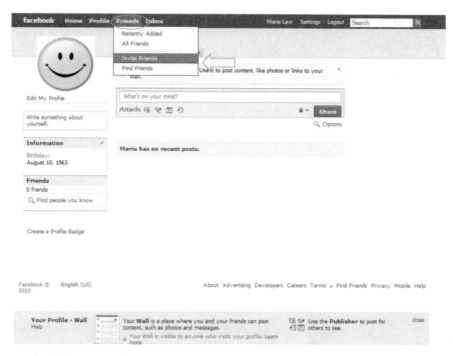

Figure 13-15. Selecting "Friends" from the Facebook menu bar.

Once you've gotten your privacy settings in place, return to the main screen. You can invite friends by selecting "friends" from the option in the blue menu bar.

Figure 13-16.

Like LinkedIn, Facebook offers similar tools for inviting friends from your contacts list in your email box

In Appendix E, you'll find instructions on setting up a Facebook Fan Page, as well as information on importing your blog content to your fan page wall.

CHAPTER THIRTEEN

Best Practices

ONCE YOU'VE ADOPTED SOCIAL media, you'll want to adopt what we refer to collectively as "best practices," which will let you maximize the effectiveness of social media tools while minimizing your time investments. Best practices we'll cover include:

- **Best Practice #1: Make time for social media through use of time management techniques and leveraging shortcuts.**
- **Best Practice #2: Delegate and outsource social media practices where appropriate.**
- **Best Practice #3: Evaluate return on investment.**
- **Best Practice #4: Guard your reputation online.**
- **Best Practice #5: Engage social media authentically. Always.**

Best Practice #1: Time Management and Leveraging Convergence Tools

Many lawyers understand the importance of networking, but let's face it—running a law practice takes time and no one ever seems to have enough of it. In fact, the lack of time is one of the main reasons lawyers offer as an excuse to avoid online networking. However, if you use the right timesaving tools, you can streamline your online networking experience, making the time you spend online more effective and efficient.

Below we discuss two topics: (1) general time management principles for participating in social media and (2) categories of tools that can help you manage and streamline your social media participation, including (1) browser tools; (2) shortcuts; (3) convergence features; and (4) mobile apps.

Overview of Time Management Concerns

Aside from blog postings (which can take time to draft), most social media does not require much time once you've made the initial investment in setting up a profile. Yet it can devolve into a time sink nonetheless. That's because even little interruptions can consume a disproportionate amount of time, indeed, far more than the activity leading to the initial interruption. Several years back, *The New York Times Magazine* described this phenomenon in its piece, "Life Hackers" (online at **http://www.nytimes.com/2005/10/16/magazine/16guru.html**):

> [A time management study by Gloria Mark, a professor at the University of California, Irvine showed that] Each employee spent only 11 minutes on any given project before being interrupted and whisked off to do something else. What's more, each 11-minute project was itself fragmented into even shorter three-minute tasks, like answering email messages, reading a Web page or working on a spreadsheet. And each time a worker was distracted from a task, it would take, on average, 25 minutes to return to that task. To perform an office job today, it seems, your attention must skip like a stone across water all day long, touching down only periodically.

Yet even as overuse of social media can result in lost time, underuse has its drawbacks as well. Sometimes lawyers get so consumed with trials or briefs that they vanish from the social media scene entirely, giving rise to an inconsistent presence that can reduce the effectiveness of social media. Below, we offer tips from time management experts, as well as from our own experience, that will enable lawyers to maintain a constant, robust social media presence without taking too big a bite out of their busy schedule.

How Much Time Will I Need?

Before you can manage your time on social media, you should estimate how much time you'll need to spend on a daily or weekly basis to achieve your goals. Getting started on most platforms will involve a greater time commitment because you'll need to set up and stock your profiles.

It's tough to generalize how much time a lawyer should devote to social media. Much of the calculation depends upon the lawyer's goals, selected social media tool, and intended use. For example, a lawyer who wants to meet more colleagues in the pharmaceutical industry might spend thirty minutes to an hour a day monitoring LinkedIn, responding to questions, and exploring new contacts. By contrast, a lawyer who markets to consumer clients may check his LinkedIn profile once a month. In addition, some goals may require more time to achieve. For example, a lawyer who starts a blog with the goal of establishing a reputation as an East Coast civil rights litigator may need to spend an hour a day, several days a week to produce content for the blog—and to continue blogging for four to five months to gain traction with potential readers.

Budget more time rather than less when stepping foot into social media—anywhere from four to eight hours per week, inclusive of blog posts (which, along with any video you choose to create and upload, will prove the most time consuming), to respond to questions on directory sites, to interact on Twitter, and to redistribute content. Again, these are only very rough guidelines. If you can't spare that much time, limit your engagement to just one or two social media platforms and accomplish as much as you can in the time available. On the other hand, if you're just starting out in the law or as a solo practitioner and you have more time on your hands than money, you can't go wrong putting your energy into social media to establish expertise and develop professional relationships.

Another way to save time and use social media efficiently is to use your smart phone to update your status and interact on social media.

The use of mobile phones to access the Internet and social media has increased greatly in recent years and this trend is only expected to increase exponentially as more and more people acquire smart phones. In fact, it is predicted that by 2013, more people will access the Web from a hand-held device than a PC.[1]

As discussed in the "Mobile Tools" section that follows, most major social networks, such as LinkedIn, Facebook and Twitter, can be accessed via your smart phone using specific applications made for that purpose.

Facebook and LinkedIn offer specific mobile interfaces along with applications that you can download to your phone. There are a number of different Twitter applications that can be used as more fully described in the "Twitter Tools" section that follows.

It makes sense to use down time during a commute or while waiting for your client's case to be called to engage on social media. Doing so simply makes sense—it's an efficient use of your time and allows you to take advantage of what would otherwise be wasted down time.

---

[1] http://www.gartner.com/it/page.jsp?id=1278413

Calendar Blocks of Time

Social media is best accomplished in blocks. Set aside a block of time at the beginning or end of the day to post Tweets, blog posts, and status updates. (Note: some experts recommend that you not log on to social media first thing in the morning unless you are disciplined enough to pull away, and instead, suggest checking in only after you've accomplished one piece of substantive work.) It's important that you calendar for social media and incorporate it into your routine so that you're more likely to stick to it when your schedule gets busy.

Take a Batch Approach

When it comes to writing blog posts, discipline yourself to write in batches and then auto post them throughout the week. Incrementally, there's only marginally more time involved in writing three blog posts all at once rather than one. You can batch other activity as well—such as stocking up on ideas for posts or responding to answers on LinkedIn or Avvo.

Squeeze Social Media Activity Into the Cracks

Let's face it, social media isn't rocket science and rarely requires your full brain to engage. So save social media for spare minutes—like waiting in carpool lines at your kids' school or at the clerk's office at court—when you can catch up in a hurry. (That's why mobile apps, discussed below, are so important.) You can even participate in social media while watching television with the family or while your kids do their homework because it doesn't demand your full attention.

Time Management Tips on Social Media from a Time Management Expert

Bill Jawitz

TimeSavvyAttorneys.com

Of Fractals and Food Shopping: Managing Your Social Media Time Effectively

Like a fractal, which can be magnified to reveal the same structural pattern at both the micro and macro levels, your approach to managing your social media activities will reflect your overall approach to managing your time. If you're a strong time manager, the guidelines presented here will be fairly easy to follow. If you're not, you'll pick up some tips that will help you manage all of your time more effectively, including your social media time.

On to metaphor number two: we all know that going food shopping without a list is not as effective as going *with* a list. Without a list, it takes longer, you get things you don't need (and you forget things you *do* need), and you often spend more money than necessary. Why? Because you're wandering, trying to rely on your memory, and buying on impulse.

The combined implication here? Improving your overall time management skills will help you more effectively manage your social media time, and following a game plan will make that time more efficient and more profitable.

The first step is to develop a positive mindset about this still-new—and fast-evolving—phenomenon. Many lawyers are hesitant to allocate consistent time building their social media presence because they:

♦ don't have enough understanding of the various processes involved

♦ had initially unrealistic expectations about results and then gave up after a few months

♦ are not convinced of the ROI (return on investment) they'll receive

♦ have heard horror stories from other people about time wasted on social media

♦ are generally risk-averse and the thought of publishing widely distributed content on the Internet is threatening

♦ find it too hard to find good content on a regular basis

♦ find it too hard to come up with a fresh perspective or unique voice

Here are the top seven tactics for creating that positive mindset and spending the right amount of time on your social media activities.

1. Establish Activity Targets

Set targets for the number of actions to take each week, and block out time for them on your calendar. These might be the number of blog posts you'll read—or write, or comment on. Or tweets you'll post, or forward. Or how many JD Supra articles you'll look at. Or how many LinkedIn profiles you'll review.

It's good practice to allocate roughly one quarter of your social media time to research and reading, one half to writing content, and the last quarter to engaging your readers/followers by forwarding and/or commenting on useful content from others.

Finally, since you can't master all social media channels at once no matter how motivated you are, consider focusing on one or two major SM channels each quarter: Q1: LinkedIn and JD Supra; Q2: Facebook; Q3: Blogs; Q4: Twitter.

2. Be Smart About Learning the Basics

- Find a college kid or law school student to teach you the basics
- Use YouTube to find video tutorials on how to accomplish a particular social media task
- Use the "Help" or "Learning Center" features of the various social media sites

3. Schedule Time and Set Limits

Allocate specific time on specific days for your social media activities and use reminders and alarms to signal when to stop.

4. Avoid Social Media as Procrastination

Notice the little voice in your head when you're using social media to avoid doing something else. It is no different than when you use other activities to procrastinate, such as revising a contract for the seventh time because you'd rather not file your expense report.

5. Systemize Your Processes

- Use Google alerts to find things to forward, comment on, or write about
- Use a writing formula such as the Content Catalyst model to methodically generate engaging articles (**http://www.designto sellonline.com/Contentcatalyst.cfm**)
- Set up an Excel spreadsheet with the "LEN" function to automatically count characters so you instantly know how long your tweet drafts are
- Create subfolders and rules in Outlook to automatically route your social media-related email.

6. Employ Software Utilities to Automate and Leverage Your Actions

- Use tools like HootSuite (**www.hootsuite.com**) to pre-schedule tweets (you can batch a whole bunch and load them up to go out over time)

- Use RoboForm (**www.roboform.com**) to securely capture and store all of your logins and form-fill information for one-click access to all of your sites
- Use a micro recorder or JOTT (**www.jott.com**) to capture your ideas when you're out and about (JOTT lets you call an 800 number and sends a transcript and the audio file of your call to your email)

7. Delegate Tasks to a Social Media Assistant
Hire an SMVA (social media virtual assistant) contractor via **www.Guru.com** or **www.Elance.com** to chop up your longer files (print or audio) and put them into smaller blog posts, podcasts, etc. SMVAs can also manage all of your content distribution.

Other lawyers see me on Facebook and Twitter all the time and have teased me about whether I get any work done, which clearly isn't the image that I want to convey. Any thoughts on how to engage lawyers and potential clients without appearing that it's all I do?

We agree that a constant presence on social media can have negative connotations. That said, there's much you can do to keep your image prominent without having others think that it's all you do. For starters, establish regular usage times. Mornings are usually liveliest on sites like Twitter, a time when many users log in to check up on stories of the day. Updating Facebook or posting on your blog are also good morning activities, again because that's when most other users come online for a daily dose of news. Establishing a regular presence at a certain time—almost like "office hours"—will let others know when to expect you. In addition to a morning log-in, you might come back on in the evening, when the mood is generally more relaxed and when it's clear to others that you're posting on your own time rather than during the work day. The same is true for weekends—and in fact, you're likely to see the most back-and-forth on sites like Twitter since participants aren't working.

Beyond making two strategic appearances, feel free to silently monitor social media sites throughout the day if you wish, so that you don't fall behind on news or other events. But unless you learn of important developments that demand immediate response or if you're killing time at the airport or carpool line, limit your midday postings to avoid a perception that you've got too much time on your hands.

Shortcut Tools

Browser tools

Firefox and Firefox add-ons   The first thing you need to do is use Firefox as your default Web browser. The tools that you can add to the browser bar will make your online life much simpler.

Our first recommendation is to ditch Google Reader as your RSS feed reader and switch to Feedly (**www.feedly.com**). Feedly pulls the feeds you subscribe to using Google Reader and presents them to you in a far more user-friendly interface. Your feeds appear in a "magazine-like" view that is much easier on the eyes and sorting through new items is simple and intuitive.

Feedly doesn't stop there, however. Feedly also allows you to quickly and easily share blogs posts and articles that appear in your feed. Choose the appropriate button in the toolbar appearing at the top of each item in your feed and, with the click of a button, you can: (1) share the content on Twitter or Facebook—Feedly automatically creates the body of the post and shortens the link for you; (2) email the content to a client or colleague to whom it might be of interest; (3) add it to your Delicious bookmarks; or (4) clip it to Evernote.

Feedly also has a new experiment, called "Karma," which lets you track links that you've shared on Twitter. You can see which links are the most popular, how many times people have "retweeted" your links, and how many times people clicked through to the content.

Finally, even when you're not reading feeds from inside the Feedly platform and are browsing the Web, Feedly allows you to share content using a mini-toolbar that appears at the very bottom left corner of each Web page. You can share a page via email, should you come across something that might be interesting to a client or a colleague. You can also post links to Twitter as you visit pages on the Web.

Another one of our favorite tools, Shareaholic (**www.shareaholic.com/**), is also a Firefox browser toolbar add-on. Like Feedly, Shareaholic automatically generates the body of each post and shortens links, thus allowing you to quickly share content on different Web platforms. One of the benefits of Shareaholic is the breadth of networking sites that it supports, including Twitter, Facebook, LinkedIn, Friendfeed, Digg, Reddit, StumbleUpon, Evernote, Delicious, Diigo, and Twine. With the click of a button you can instantly share information with your connections across the Web.

Twitter tools

Twitter can be a time sink if you don't use it correctly. Fortunately, there are also a number of useful tools that can make your user experience much simpler and more efficient should you decide to test the waters and begin interacting on Twitter.

As discussed in previous chapters, Twitter can be quite useful for many lawyers. Twitter allows you to network with other lawyers across the country and the world, promote your practice and its website or other online presence, receive news updates relevant to your area of practice, and connect with potential clients or referral sources.

At first glance, Twitter seems like anything but the wonderful tool that it is. However, rest assured, Twitter can be an invaluable resource, as long as you know how to use it. The first step is to create an account at Twitter.com. Make sure to choose a username that is easily recognizable and promotes your practice.

The next step is to locate people and organizations you'd like to follow, including people you already know, those who practice in the same area of law, potential clients, and users with similar personal interests. There are a number of ways to do this.

Locate people you already know by running your Web-hosted email address through Twitter's system. (You'll be prompted to do so when you first sign up.) Once you've connected with people you know, check their follower lists and "follow" anyone who interests you.

In addition to Twitter lists, which are conveniently organized at Listorious (**www.listorious.com**), online directories, such as Twellow (**www.twellow .com**), also categorize Twitter users for you by occupation, interests, location, etc. Review the directory to locate people with whom you'd like to connect.

You also can search Twitter using Twitter's built-in search function to locate people who are discussing topics that interest you. For example, if you're interested in wine, you can run a search for "wine" and other wine-related terms to locate other oenophiles.

Once you've set up an account and connected with a few people, start Tweeting about your day-to-day law practice, your firm's blog or other online presence, news of interest to you and your followers, and any other topics that interest you.

Engage in conversations with other users by responding to their Tweets. Simply type "@username," then add your comment. Retweet other users' tweets that you believe may be of interest to your followers by typing "RT @username" and the content of the tweet.

There are a number of platforms and tools available that can make your Twitter experience far more pleasant. Three desktop Twitter platforms that are very popular are Tweetdeck (**www.tweetdeck.com**), Seesmic (**www.seesmic.com/**), and Tweetie (**www.atebits.com/tweetie-mac/**). These platforms offer different features that simplify your Twitter user experience. Tweetree (**www.tweetree.com**) and Tweetvisor (**www.tweet visor.com**) are two online Web interfaces that accomplish the same goal of making Twitter more user-friendly.

Convergence Features

Fortunately, most social media providers are sensitive to concerns about "social media overload" and have developed what we refer to as "convergence applications," which help users coordinate their presence across a variety of social media platforms. Setting up most convergence applications either requires inserting a widget on your site or inputting the URL from your blog into a toolbar that will extract some or all of the posts and redistribute them.

For example, you can add a widget, like sharethis.com, to your blog to distribute a specific post to Facebook or Twitter (as well as to other sites, such as Digg.com or Stumbleupon.com, which aggregate recommendations about blog posts, videos, or other online materials submitted by users).

You can also set up your Facebook profile to import the feed from your blogs, as discussed in Chapter 9.

There are so many different convergence tools, with more emerging all the time, that we can't cover all of them here. Essentially, the rules for

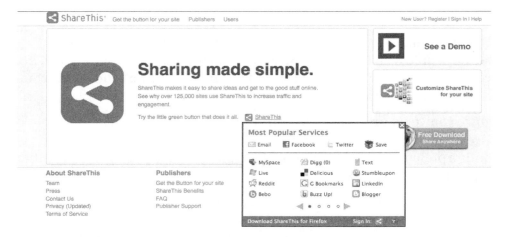

Figure 14-1. This screenshot shows the sharethis.com site. To see a list of sites where you can share blog posts, click on the small "Share this icon" and the box of options (shown above) will appear. For step-by-step instructions for installing ShareThis on your blog or website, go to the "Customize ShareThis" for your site button on the right side of the page.

choosing convergence tools parallel the rules for choosing social media applications: first, identify your target audience and goals, then identify tools to serve those needs. For example, if one of your goals is to engage and connect with clients and colleagues, you might post your Twitter feeds to Facebook, so that your friends who aren't on Twitter can get a sense of what you're up to. Likewise, if you want to showcase your reputation as a clever brief-writer, employ convergence tools that will redistribute legal pleadings that you've uploaded to sites like JD Supra or Docstoc.

Understandably, some lawyers are skeptical about the value of convergence tools. After all, why would your childhood friends who aren't lawyers want to read your recent blog post on the ins and outs of filing a personal injury suit in Nebraska? Perhaps they don't, but making the posts available is a way of educating and explaining to your friends what you do on a day-to-day basis, just as you might talk about your job if you had lunch face-to-face. Moreover, helping friends understand what you do enables them to send you better qualified leads.

Below, we provide several examples of convergence tools that are popular with lawyers. We simply don't have the space to provide details on how to install every tool, but we've linked to sites where you can find instructions beneath the screenshots below. Additionally, in Part IV we'll show you

Figure 14-2. This screen shot of the Connecticut Employment Law Blog includes a "Share Link" that allows the author to distribute individual posts to Twitter, LinkedIn, Facebook, and other social media platforms. The tool is accessible beneath each blog post.

how to activate some of the convergence tools that are available when you set up a user profile on Facebook or LinkedIn.

You can also use Twitter applications on your smart phone to keep up with the conversation stream. Popular iPhone Twitter applications

Figure 14-3. Twitterfeed.com allows you to feed your blog feed to Twitter and Facebook. Twitterfeed will automatically stream links to all of your blog posts, so if you blog several times a day, keep in mind that a constant stream of links to your social media sites might be annoying. A tool like ShareThis might be a better alternative because you can select specific posts to share on a case-by-case basis.

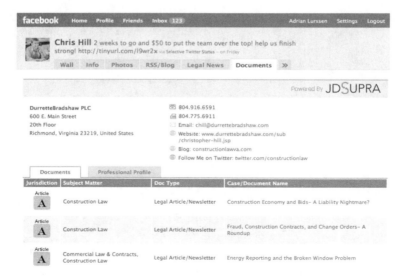

Figure 14-4. JD Supra offers a Facebook app that enables you to share documents that you've posted on JD Supra with Facebook friends. JD Supra offers instructions on how to install the JD Supra App: **http://scoop.jdsupra.com/2009/10/articles/jd-supra-updates/ tip-how-to-install-apps-on-facebook-pages/**.

Figure 14-5. The Mashtag Blog, run by Bottomlinelawgroup.com displays the author's Twitter stream in the right hand column. Wordpress and other blog platforms offer several widgets that you can install to display your tweets on your blog.

include Tweetie (**www.tweetie.com**), Tweetdeck (**www.tweetdeck.com**) and Twitterific (**www.twitterific.com**).

Arguably, the most popular BlackBerry application is Twitterberry (**www.twitterberry.com**). Other BlackBerry applications to consider are Twibble (**www.twibble.com**) and Tiny Tweeter (**www.tinytweeter.com**).

If the Palm Pre is your smart phone of choice, Tweed (**http://tweed.pivotal labs.com/**) is a good Twitter application to use.

Use these tools and you'll find that your time spent on Twitter is simple and effective.

Integration and Convergence Tools

As mentioned in Part II, most social media sites have developed applications that effectively let you get "double duty" out of postings—for example, they circulate blog posts to Twitter or pull your Twitter feeds on to your blog. Using these convergence tools regularly will save you time and allow you to supercharge the value of the time that you spend on social media activities.

Mobile Tools

What better place to engage social media than while waiting on a line at the clerk's office or sitting in the carpool lane to pick up your kids? Those slivers of time aren't long enough to draft a brief (and might not be quiet enough time to allow you to return a phone call), but they're ideal for catching up on social media.

You can find a variety of mobile apps, either developed by a social media company itself or an independent provider, which you can download to your smart phone. Most of the apps are free or very inexpensive, so you can experiment with a few until you find one that fits your needs. Below are a couple of examples of the mobile apps available for "the big three" social media platforms.

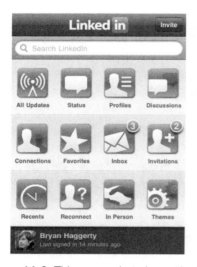 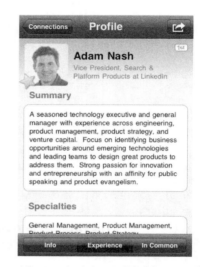

Figure 14-6. This screenshot shows the LinkedIn mobile app for iphone 3.0. Menu options are on the screen at left; the screen at right shows how a profile displays. You can use LinkedIn mobile to connect with other users, update your profile, or check out profiles of people whom you may be en route to meet. LinkedIn also has a mobile app for Palm Pre and, in November 2009, announced an upcoming release of a LinkedIn app for the Blackberry, though it has not been released as of the date this book went to press.

Figure 14-7. Facebook has developed many mobile options which you can access directly from **www.facebook.com/mobile**. The mobile apps offer many of the same features as Facebook, including the ability to directly upload a photo taken on your phone to your Facebook page.

Figure 14-8. In December 2009, Twitter released a new mobile version. Prior to that time, users looking to keep up with Twitter by phone relied on third-party developed applications, like Tweetie, Twittelator, and Tweetdeck for iphone. All of these apps support Twitter's core features; they allow you to send a tweet, follow a user, retweet and direct message.

Best Practice #2: Outsourcing Social Media—Rewards and Risks

You may be tempted to "outsource" your online networking to save time, but, generally speaking, the key to online networking is to interact with your connections in a genuine, transparent manner. Outsourcing that interaction undermines the very basis of a successful social media participation.

What You Can Outsource

There are, however, certain tasks that can be outsourced successfully. For example, you can hire a company to design and install a blog and create a logo and design that you can use for various platforms. Setting up a profile can be onerous, particularly when you have several years of work experience, multiple articles, and speaking engagements to include. If you compile all of the information, you can delegate profile creation to an assistant. An assistant can also update your profiles to keep them current.

You can also use an assistant to upload documents to JD Supra, post to your blog or other social media platforms about recent law firm achievements, locate topics for blog posts, and monitor mentions of your firm or topics of interest through Google alerts.

What You Shouldn't Outsource

Some lawyers hire ghostwriters to write their blogs or professional copywriters who will draft a social media bio or write "SEO enhanced" copy for your blog (i.e., copy that contains keywords that your target audience will use to find you). When it comes to blogging, we don't necessarily recommend this practice, but we recognize that busy lawyers won't always have the time to prepare fresh content for a blog. Alternatively, you could invite guest posters or hire a new law graduate or law student to research and author posts with you for your blog or even publish posts under their own byline.

Likewise, to get the most out of your online participation, the actual online interaction with other users should be done by you. You are the "face" of your firm and social networking is all about connecting with other people. Therefore, in order to achieve the best results, we recommend that you write your blog posts and respond to comments about the post. You should post in forums and respond to the comments that follow your original post. You should be responsible for your status posts and interactions with others on Twitter, Facebook, and LinkedIn.

"For blogging, you can start writing yourself, or if you find you don't have the time, consider hiring a temp or someone with blogging experience. Give them specific instructions on what to blog about (court filings, news related to personal injury, intellectual property, etc), and be clear that you reserve the right to make edits. It might take a few tries, but if the blogger is any good, he or she will be able to find topics on his or own and pick up the nuances or points you want to make. Not only will that help take some of the pressure off, but it will also help build your online credibility and improve your search engine rankings."

—*Gwynne Monahan, Founder & Chief Consultant, Shadow Froggy Consulting; Founder, Lawyer Connection*

How a Virtual Assistant Can Help A Lawyer With Social Media.

By Tina Marie Hilton of *Clerical Advantage*

The word is out. Attorneys can no longer ignore social media marketing. Clients are no longer using traditional avenues like the Yellow Pages to find a lawyer. You know all that right? The question isn't *if* you should be involved in social media, but how can you find the time to do it and run your practice too. The answer could lie in the use of a virtual assistant.

A virtual assistant is an experienced professional providing specialized services from their office to yours, via the use of technology. Many virtual assistants, or VA's as they are sometimes called, not only have experience with these social media technologies, but use them for their own businesses. And best of all, they can help you get your social media presence on track while you focus on practicing law.

What type of tasks can you outsource to a virtual assistant? Just about anything. But since we're discussing social media specifically, I've listed just a few ways a VA can help you with social media support.

♦ A virtual assistant can check the meta data in your website, research the keywords you're using, and make sure the proper keywords are integrated not just in your meta data, but more importantly in your website copy and blog.

♦ Speaking of a blog, a virtual assistant can help you set up your blog, as well as assisting you in keeping it up to date with services like shadow blogging, where they can take your basic post and add all of the important things like images, formatting, and then post it for you. They can also be put in charge of administering your comments, letting you know when a comment requires your response.

♦ A virtual assistant can help you to connect your target market via social media by setting up your social media profiles (Twitter, LinkedIn, Facebook Page, etc.). Then they can connect them to your website and each other.

♦ A virtual assistant can set your blog up so that every time a new post goes live, an announcement and link appear on your social media sites as well.

♦ Involved in a special event? Have a virtual assistant set up the event (discuss events in your Facebook section and show screen shot) on your Facebook Page or add a page to your blog.

♦ Monitor your online reputation. Have a virtual assistant use monitoring tools to keep track of what's being said about you online and send you reports.

It's easy to become overwhelmed by the thought of practicing law and juggling the social media ball. Instead of stressing and trying to do it all, outsource social media tasks to a virtual assistant. You'll be glad you did.

Caution About Outsourcing

Outsourcing marketing = outsourcing ethics
—New York Personal Injury Attorney Blogger Eric Turkewitz

As a lawyer, the buck stops with you. You can outsource social media tasks, but at the end of the day, you alone remain responsible for ensuring that these tasks are undertaken in an ethically compliant manner. For example, let's say that you hire a marketing company to set up a blog for you and ghost write posts under your name. If it turns out that those posts violate your state's advertising rules, you're responsible for the infractions. Likewise, if an overly aggressive "social media" guru routinely annoys your Facebook friends with announcements about upcoming firm events or self-promotional wall posts, it's your reputation that suffers, not your marketer's.

Before outsourcing any social media tasks, you should educate yourself on appropriate social media protocols so that you can instruct and monitor the person you've selected to assist you with implementing a social media plan. In addition, poke around the Web to get a sense of how potential outsourcing candidates implement social media themselves. Are their communications authentic and personable or tacky and "salesy"? Chances are that they'll use similar tactics to help you engage in social media as they do for themselves, so if you don't like those techniques look elsewhere.

Bear in mind that many social media marketers have a tendency to inflate their credentials and results. You may want to run some Google searches to obtain more objective information about their qualifications.

Best Practice #3: Evaluating Social Media Return on Investment (ROI) and Effectiveness

Traditional Analysis of Return on Investment

As with any marketing activity, lawyers must measure their return on investment (ROI) from social media. (For those unfamiliar with the term, ROI represents the ratio of money gained or lost in relationship to dollars spent.) But how to do it? Most social media involves an expenditure of time, not money, and many of the benefits—from increased visibility to enhanced relationships with other lawyers—don't produce measurable benefits.

Moreover, in contrast to a Yellow Pages ad, which serves the sole purpose of client generation, social media supports a wide range of goals. Thus, when calculating ROI, lawyers must consider social media's effectiveness in helping lawyers accomplish all of their goals, rather than simply focusing on whether social media resulted in more clients and revenues.

To evaluate the effectiveness of social media, we propose some metrics below.

Visitor statistics

Most blogs offer analytics where you can view how visitors arrived at your site. Are visitors coming via Twitter, Facebook, or other social media links? If so, then social media is working for SEO purposes by increasing traffic to your site.

In addition, what kinds of searches are bringing lawyers to your site? Are they the keyword strings by which you want visitors to find you? Or are they simply random search terms? If the former is true, then again your social media activities may be working by increasing the visibility of targeted keywords in Google, and also increasing the quality of leads generated.

Finally, you should always ask callers (whether they're prospective clients, reporters, or colleagues) how they've found you online—through a blog, a Google search, or social media? Their responses will give you an idea of the tools that are producing the most returns for your practice.

Call conversion rate

Have you noticed any changes in your conversion rates since you started your social media campaign? For example, are you getting the same or even fewer calls, but converting a larger percentage of those calls (and larger number overall) into clients? If so, it may be that social media tools like blogs, online documents, and a Facebook fan page are helping to educate potential clients and referral sources, thereby cutting down on inquiries from prospects who have matters that you don't handle.

More publicity

Have you noticed more inquiries from the press arriving through Twitter or your blog? Again, that's another sign that your social media campaign is making inroads and helping you increase your visibility and enhance your reputation.

Comparative costs

You can't really claim that social media is effective (or at least, cost effective) if there are less expensive alternatives that produce the same results. For example, let's say that a firm spends $1,000 per month to maintain its blog (assuming indirect costs like server space and tech support and salary for associates who write the posts) and generates one interview each month in the trade press. However, before the firm started blogging, it spent $300 a month on a PR service that generated the same one interview per month result. In this situation, the PR service is more cost effective than the blog, at least to accomplish the goal of enhanced reputation (as defined by number of media appearances).

At the same time, a firm may realize additional value from the blog that the PR service does not provide. The blog may result in more calls from existing clients with questions and additional work related to topics that your firm covers at its blog. So while the blog may lose points for effectiveness on the PR side, it may gain points for contributing to client development.

Best Practice #4: Guarding Your Reputation Online

Guard Your Reputation as Zealously as You Represent Clients

Perhaps the most important step that lawyers can take to avoid fallout from negative information is to continuously and vigorously monitor their respective online reputations. If that sounds time-consuming, it doesn't have to be. In fact, by implementing a few simple procedures, you can monitor your social media presence in just 10 to 15 minutes a day. Here's how:

♦ Check Twitter for tweets about your company and using search tools like Tweetdeck or TwitterSearch to monitor conversations in realtime;

♦ Set Google Alerts for your name or those of cases or client matters you're working on;

♦ Look for questions to answer on LinkedIn (answering questions can increase positive search engine visibility); and

♦ Use Google to track other social networking sites and, in particular, blogs, where a colleague may have criticized a posting or commented negatively on the way in which you handled a case.

In addition to these general social networking sites, lawyers should regularly monitor sites like Avvo and other similar sites where clients are permitted to post ratings, comment, or review lawyers. And don't forget to keep an eye on sites like LinkedIn, where colleagues can post testimonials.

If You Find Something Positive, Reinforce It

Of course, lawyers are most interested in dealing with negative information. However, even when you find positive comments, you should respond with a thank you. Clients and colleagues who take the time to praise something you've done can serve as your greatest allies if you ever need to undertake damage control against unfair criticism or unflattering commentary. Take the time to cultivate a group of colleagues who can monitor the Internet for you and go on the offensive when you discover damaging information.

Dealing with Negative Information

So what can you do if you uncover negative or unflattering information about yourself? First, if comments are anonymous or located on an unpopular site that doesn't get much traffic, then ignoring the information might make the most sense. However, if negative information comes up high in search engine results, then, credible or not, you've probably got to take some action. First, you can step up your online activity at your blog, which should generate positive search results—that will hopefully relegate the negative information several pages back in a Google search. But you'll also need to take more direct action, such as responding to the negative commentary either on the offender's blog or at the site where the comments are located.

You could also consider contacting the site owner and asking for removal of the information. In many cases, a site owner will be accommodating where negative commentary is posted by a third party. However, most bloggers who write a criticism will be reluctant to remove it; perhaps the best you can hope for is an opportunity to lodge a response. You may also want to take the opportunity to explain a situation head-on. In some instances, past grievance decisions against lawyers are available online for clients to discover. You may be better off acknowledging a grievance or suspension and explaining it rather than letting clients discover it for themselves. It's true that this approach is risky as you might draw more attention to the grievance than if you'd just let it alone. On the other hand, if you believe that the grievance has so much prominence that it's driving away business, you really have nothing to lose.

Defamatory information

Sometimes, you may find information that isn't just unflattering but downright defamatory. In that situation, consult with a defamation lawyer to obtain an objective opinion. This is one type of case where you don't want to represent yourself because if you overreact, your response will attract more attention than the underlying information. In the event that you're able to convince or compel your detractor to take down defamatory material, be sure to submit a removal request form to Google (through **https://www.google.com/webmasters/tools/removals?pli=1**) so that the site doesn't linger in Google's cache.

Conclusion

As use of social media, Web 2.0, and user-generated content and applications increase, so too does the potential for negative commentary regarding our work as lawyers. Essentially, we lawyers have no choice: We can either monitor, and strategically address, what's written and how it impacts to our reputation . . . or not. Withdrawing from or avoiding social media altogether makes the problem worse because it won't stop the attacks and leaves us defenseless. For that reason alone, lawyers should engage social media—if not to attract business, then to guard against losing it.

Best Practice #5: Authentic Engagement

One of the most powerful benefits of social media is its ability to help lawyers build richer and more trusted relationships with colleagues, clients, and other lawyers. Eventually, these relationships may yield financial benefits in the form of referrals and business, not to mention personal satisfaction and a sense of community. Yet social media won't produce these benefits if participants don't act authentically when they engage social media.

According to Wikipedia, "**Authenticity**" refers to "the truthfulness of origins, attributions, commitments, sincerity, devotion, and intentions." Put more simply, authenticity online means not only just being yourself, but also presenting yourself to others honestly and transparently.

So don't exaggerate your accomplishments or lie about your experience. Share your positive experiences on Twitter, but don't be a braggart or a blowhard. Find your own voice and use it at your blog instead of hiring a ghostwriter (of course, if you're too busy to blog, you could use a law student to write posts, but if you do, disclose it). Express your opinions even if they're unpopular. And even in a twenty-first century world, don't be ashamed to let "old fashioned values" like your passion for the law and justice, your quest for excellence, and your work ethic shine through. Most of all, instead of trying to create an online persona—an inspirational image of who you'd like to be—just be yourself.

Of course, being yourself doesn't compel you to disclose everything. There is, after all, such a thing as TMI (too much information). In addition, if you're a private person who's not inclined to chat about family on Facebook or tweet about your favorite pair of shoes, then don't feel compelled to share.

Finally, like it or not, as a lawyer, you have little choice but to engage social media authentically since our code of professional ethics prohibits deceptive or misleading conduct. So for example, a female lawyer who portrays herself on social media as "A Dad Who Represents Dads" in order to market to fathers involved in custody battles, isn't just acting inauthentic, she's most likely violating ethics rules as well.

CHAPTER FOURTEEN

Social Media Concerns Unique to Large Firms and Trial Lawyers

A year ago (a law firm) commissioned a song celebrating (their nomination as one of the best companies to work for). . .

The law blog "Above the Law" put the song on YouTube.

Merriment ensued.

Then (the firm) found out that people were laughing at them.

So, they laughed and said "Yeah, it is a silly song."

No, of course not.

So they started to act like a bunch of lawyers.

They sent YouTube a DMCA takedown notice. YouTube took it down.

That got (the firm) some attention. . .

Heck, nobody was even sure it was real. Until they lawyered up.

—YouTube video commentary
**(http://www.youtube.com/watch?v=7SeL6i3sHM0&feature=PlayList&p
=BEA63222CFE1FEA8&playnext=1&playnext_from=PL&index=11***)*
(66,637 views as of 11/09)

PR Considerations for Large Law Firms

A few years ago, very few lawyers knew what a "blog" was. And, quite frankly, most didn't really care. Time has a way of changing things. The increasing popularity of social media, including the indisputable and viral effect of blogs, has finally caused those at the top of the legal profession to sit up and take notice.

The major impetus behind this change has been a number of notable public relations disasters occurring over the last few years involving large law firms. Unfortunately, these firms, at the time, were unfamiliar with the social media landscape.

The most notable incident, described above, involved Nixon Peabody's rather lawyerly response to the leak of a celebratory song commissioned by the firm. In another case, a disgruntled associate's parting email to her former employer, Paul Hastings, was leaked on the Internet, causing untold amounts of negative publicity for the firm.

These and other online public relations gaffes by large law firms have forced the legal profession to reluctantly acknowledge the existence and importance of blogs and other online social media. Many large law firms are now painfully cognizant of the viral effects of online media.

The Domino's Pizza incident from 2009 is a great example of how to handle a situation that has the potential to quickly spiral out of control. Unbeknownst to higher-ups at the company, low-level employees made a video, and then posted it on YouTube. In the video, they contaminated food prior to placing it in sandwiches to be served to the public. The video went viral overnight, racking up thousands of views, comments, and blog posts. The situation had the potential to become a PR nightmare for Domino's.

In less than 24 hours, Domino's CEO recorded a video response that was posted on YouTube in which he condemned the employees' actions. His response can be viewed here: **http://www.youtube.com/watch?v= 7I6AJ49xNSQ**. This quick, timely response using the very medium that brought the scandal to light was extremely effective.

Domino's was rudely and abruptly drawn into the social media spotlight, but wisely consulted people who understood social media. Their video response to an unfortunate situation was very effective, turning what could have become a PR nightmare into a small blip on the radar.

Large law firms are inherently vulnerable to this type of social media exposure because of their size and prominence. Large firms are obvious targets and people take notice when a scandalous or embarrassing incident involving a large firm comes to light.

Accordingly, as soon as an embarrassing story breaks and blogs such as Gawker (**http://gawker.com**) or Above the Law (**http://abovethelaw.com**)

get their hands on it, an immediate response is required. For that reason, large law firms must employ people who understand social media.

If an incident occurs that is embarrassing and has the potential to go viral, a swift, targeted social media campaign is necessary. It will be much easier to implement an effective campaign if there are key people in your organization who understand and are familiar with the inner workings of social media.

Social Media Invades the Workplace

Undoubtedly, your employees are participating in social media, whether you're aware of it or not. Imposing a blanket prohibition against social media use at work is as unrealistic as it is ineffective. It's inevitable: your employees are going to use social networks both at work and at home regardless of your attempts to curtail their use.

As discussed in detail previously, social media is a phenomenon that is here to stay. Forbidding social media use is a losing proposition. A more sensible course of action is to set reasonable limits on the use of social media sites while at work and create a social media policy that is simple and effective.

Indisputably, social media use can be addictive and can reduce workers' productivity. For that reason it makes sense to limit the amount of time that your employees are permitted to spend engaging in social media while at work. Businesses are addressing this issue in a number of ways. For example, one of the authors of this book recently read an article which described a business that permitted its employees to choose to take either a cigarette break or a social media break—many people chose the latter. Giving employees this choice gives them a sense of empowerment and is a creative way to address this issue.

All law firms should have a social media policy in place. The policy need not be complicated, but rather, should set forth general guidelines that must be followed by all employees in a way that is easily understandable by all employees at all levels. A simple, well-written policy provides employees with guidance as to appropriate online behavior and emphasizes the consequences of inappropriate behavior.

An effective social media policy should indicate the consequence if a violation occurs and should encourage employees to exercise good judgment and common sense when interacting online. Employees should be advised that they have no reasonable expectation of privacy regarding electronic communications in the workplace and should be required to sign consent forms regarding workplace and work equipment monitoring. Employees should be advised that electronic communications consisting of unlawful, discriminatory activities or that are contrary to the law firm's interests are forbidden.

For an example of an effective and yet fairly simple social media policy, see the full text of Intel's social media policy at **http://www.intel.com/ sites/sitewide/en_US/social-media.htm**.

Social Media Policy Resources

- **10 Must-Haves for Your Social Media Policy:**
  http://mashable.com/2009/06/02/social-media-policy-musts/
- **Online Database of Social Media Policies:**
  http://socialmediagovernance.com/policies.php?f=0
- **Social Media Policy Templates:**
  http://socialmediagovernance.com/policies.php?f=6

Social Media Invades the Courtroom

Like large law firms, our courtrooms are no longer immune to the effects of social media. Technology is changing rapidly. Information is being exchanged online in ways not previously encountered or envisioned. A recent example of this phenomenon is the increase in the number of reporters seeking to use Twitter to report live in the midst of trials.

For example, last year in a Colorado courtroom, *Wichita Eagle* reporter Ron Sylvester sought to post to his blog and Twitter throughout the trial. Over the objections of both the prosecution and defense counsel, the trial judge allowed the use of cell phones and computers in the courtroom during the child abuse trial.

Throughout the proceedings, Sylvester chronicled the happenings of the trial. At one point, he posted on Twitter about an evidentiary issue:

- Getting ready for pretrial hearing of George Tiller, Day 2. 9:58 a.m. *yesterday from txt*
- Judge Owens has called the hearing to order. He is ruling on whether Kline has to turn over personal diary to Tiller's attorneys. 10:28 a.m. *yesterday from txt*

- Kline gets to keep his diaries private. 10:32 a.m. *yesterday from txt*
- Owens ruled that 'work product' applies to prosecutors, such as notes on opinions and theories of a case. 10:32 a.m. *yesterday from txt*

Many found it fascinating to watch the trial unfold live, as it happened, rather than reading accounts of it after the fact. Technology made that possible. Technology has invaded our lives, our homes, our offices, and our courtrooms. Technological change has made many things possible that once were unimaginable.

Likewise, astute lawyers should not overlook social media websites as a potential source of useful information for pending lawsuits. Social media sites can offer a vast array of interesting information. Litigators and matrimonial lawyers are finding that mining social networking sites for information about opposing parties and witnesses can prove to be quite beneficial.

Conclusion

Jurors are accessing the Internet during trial and Facebook statuses are being used as alibis in criminal cases; the legal implications of social media use can no longer be ignored. However, the legal profession, so fond of precedent, has always been somewhat slow to embrace change. Lawyers have traditionally balked at technological advancements and only begrudgingly adopted new technological tools when it became apparent that there was no other alternative.

Our profession's reaction to social media has been no different. Many still dismiss it as mere "child's play," a trend that is not worthy of acknowledgement or utilization. However, social media is not a fad; it's a revolution. And revolutions, quite simply, cannot be ignored. Lawyers who ignore social media and technological advancements do so to their own detriment. If you're smart, you'll join the revolution, or, at the very least, gain a basic understanding of it. Your future clients, and your bottom line, will thank you for it.

PART FIVE

The Ethical and Legal Issues of Social Media

CHAPTER FIFTEEN

The Ethics of Social Media

Avoid False and Misleading Communications in Social Media

With the recent explosion of social media applications, many state disciplinary committees have not yet had an opportunity to issue formal opinions on the ethics of social media for lawyers. Moreover, some of the early state decisions on social media, discussed in this chapter, reflect misconceptions about what social media is and how it actually works in practice.

Despite still-evolving ethics rules on social media, we believe that lawyers can embrace social media without fear of ethical repercussions. As we stated at the outset, social media changes the media of lawyer communications, not the message. Conduct that is unethical—whether violating duties of confidentiality or using deceptive tactics to solicit clients—isn't immunized merely because that conduct takes place on Facebook or via a blog. So long as lawyers engage social media responsibly, taking into account ethics rules that govern other conduct and consulting their ethics hotline or bar counsel where necessary, they can reduce the risk of ethics violations.

Many states are guided, in one way or another, by the ABA's rule regarding communication of legal services, which prohibits false or misleading communication:

Rule 7.1 Communications Concerning a Lawyer's Services

A lawyer shall not make a false or misleading communication about the lawyer or the lawyer's services. A communication is false or misleading if it contains a material misrepresentation of fact or law, or omits a fact necessary to make the statement considered as a whole not materially misleading.

The rule against false or deceptive communication should inform all lawyers' participation in social media. For example, in creating profiles, lawyers should include accurate information about past employment and accomplishments or refrain from giving testimonials about others that suggest that the lawyer is personally familiar with a colleague's work when in fact, that is not the case. Likewise, lawyers should avoid use of social media to convey false expectations about results or nonverifiable information. Later in this part, we'll discuss how certain uses of social media tools may raise concerns about false or deceptive communication.

Read the Bar Rules!

Even with the ABA rule in the backdrop, we cannot emphasize enough that it is absolutely imperative that you personally take the time to read and familiarize yourself with your jurisdiction's ethics rules governing advertising, as well as specific opinions on social media (the bars are just starting to address questions raised by social media; you'll find a summary of important cases to date at the end of this chapter). All too frequently, lawyers tend to rely on rumors that certain conduct is not permitted, when in fact, the situations at issue involved conduct in another jurisdiction, were distinguishable on their facts—or the rumor was just plain wrong.

A recent ABA Teleconference on Ethics in Web 2.0 Marketing emphasized the importance of reviewing ethics rules (**http://www.abanet.org/cle/ programs/nosearch/teiomo.html**; *see* call summary at The Lawyerist, "Legal Marketing Ethics in a Web 2.0 World," **http://lawyerist.com/2009/ 07/legal-marketing-ethics-web-2-0/** (Jul. 17, 2009)) since each jurisdiction takes a different approach. The ABA conveniently provides links to each state's advertising ethics rules to make it easy for lawyers, particularly those licensed in several jurisdictions, to review them (ABA, "Links to State Ethics Rules Governing Lawyer Advertising, Solicitation, and Marketing," **http:// www.abanet.org/legalservices/clientdevelopment/adrules/states.html**).

Understand the Categories of Conduct that May Raise Red Flags

You'd go crazy trying to memorize the specifics of every ethics rule. And we certainly can't summarize the crazy patchwork of ethics regulations for fifty different jurisdictions in one blog post. As a first step, what's more important than the specifics is the issue spotting—the ability to recognize those categories of conduct that may raise ethics red flags. Once you encounter an activity that you think may raise an ethics issue, you can review your ethics rules and any related ethics opinions to determine whether the activity is permissible. Below is a quick table of some of the types of activity that can raise red flags (for a near complete comparative analysis of ABA Model rules and state rules on advertising, *see* **http://www.abanet.org/cpr/professionalism/state-advertising.pdf**).

Comparative Chart: Ethical Obligations

Activity	Ethics problem	Sites where possibly implicated	ABA Model Code Resolution	Other bar approaches
False or misleading information		Directory sites, archiving sites	ABA Model Rule 7.1 (above—so long as not false and misleading)	Many states follow the ABA Rule. California's rule is substantially different (CA Rule 1-400).
Testimonials	Non-verifiable, misleading, no personal knowledge	Directory sites	ABA Model Rule 7.1	AR Rule 7.1(d); FL Rule 4-7.2(c)(1)(J); WY Rule 7.2(h); Utah Bar Opinion 09-01, **http://www.utah bar.org/rules_ops_pols/ ethics_opinions/op_08_03.html** (must include appropriate disclaimers).
Ratings	Can lawyer link to ratings? What if ratings are on third-party sites—can bar regulate?	Directory sites	ABA Model Rule 7.1	Connecticut (**http://www .jud.ct.gov/SGC/Adv_ opinions/Adv_07-00188 .pdf**), Alaska (**https:// www.alaskabar.org/ servlet/content/2009_02 .html**), and North Carolina (**http://www.ncbar.com/ ethics/ethics.asp?page=1 &keywords=Super+ Lawyers**), for example, allow lawyers to link to the Ratings site, but the lawyer must clarify the purpose of such sites or include appropriate disclaimers.
Endorsements from colleagues	Deceptive if lawyer gives impression he's worked with colleague and hasn't	LinkedIn, directory sites	ABA Model Rule 7.1	SC Bar, Ethics Opinion 09-10 (peer endorsements must meet all general ethics requirements related to solicitation and testimonials) (**http://www.scbar .org/member_resources/ ethics_advisory_opinions/ &id=678**).
Stating a "specialization"	Stating a specialization can be misleading	LinkedIn (has box for "specialty")	ABA Model Rule 7.4	NY Bar Rule 7.4(c); CA Rule 1-400; WY Rule 7.2(g) prohibits stating a specialization.

Activity	Ethics problem	Sites where possibly implicated	ABA Model Code Resolution	Other bar approaches
For fee referrals	Quid pro quo rec- ommendations; fee for clients	Directory sites	ABA Model Rule 7.2, but see also Rules 1.7, 1.8, and 5.4	State bar associations range from allowing for fee refer- rals from lawyers and non- lawyers to prohibiting the practice. Some bars allow it, but urge lawyers to not participate in the practice. See this ABA article for an in-depth summary, **http:// www.abanet.org/media/ youraba/200706/article11 .html**.
Client solicitation		Directory sites, blog- ging	ABA Model Rule 7.3	CA Rule 1-400 (all solicita- tion prohibited unless fam- ily member or prior profes- sional relationship, within contours of CA and US con- stitutions); NY Rule 7.3a prohibits certain forms of solicitation via "interactive computer-accessed com- munication."
Confidentiality violation	Disclosure of client information or fail- ure to adequately protect	Blogging, Twitter, JD Supra and archiving sites	ABA Model Rule 1.6, 8.3	CT Rule 1.6 (different con- ception of informed con- sent); FL Rule 4-1.6 (differ- ence between client confidences and secrets); CA 1-100, 3-100 (consid- ered by some to be the strictest confidentiality requirements).
Creating attorney- client relationship		Directory sites, blog comment sections	ABA Model Rule 1.2, 1.4, 1.16, 4.4	CO Rule 1.2; OH Rule 1.2; 7-101, 7-102, 7-106 (no direct counterpart to MR 1.2).
Ex parte	Communication with a judge outside scope of case	Facebook, community sites where lawyers can "friend" judges	ABA Model Rule 3.5(b)	
Improper contact with parties	Lawyer "friends" a defendant or communicates w/a witness	Facebook, Twitter	ABA Model Rule 3.5(b) and (c)	AZ Rule.3.5(a); courts will begin to address lawyers, judges, jurors, and parties "friending" each other (**http://nwitimes.com/ news/local/lake/article_ aa5c8a6d-a001-5882- a289-1ab8cec88214.html**).
Advertising regulations	Is a communication advertising and if so, what is required?	All forms: are they advertising and is a disclaimer or prior review required?	ABA Model Rule 7.2, 7.3(c). Traditionally, information requested by a client is not considered advertising.	NJ Rule 7.2 (all media allowed, must be mainly informational); PA Rule 7.2; CA 1-400 (no restriction on medium, and "message as a whole" will be used to determine whether decep- tive). Florida Rule 4-7.2, as amended (1/1/2010) holds that law firm websites and third-party sites like Avvo, Facebook and LinkedIn subject to Florida advertis- ing rules. Texas Rule 7.07 (LinkedIn profiles not subject to prior review of advertising rules).

Ethics of Special Forms of Social Media

Blogs

In many jurisdictions, a law firm website is considered "advertising," just like a newspaper ad or a law firm brochure. As such, a website may be subject to certain bar regulations that govern print ads, such as prior review or a requirement that the site contain a disclaimer or notice stating that the site constitutes advertising. Likewise, the same types of communications prohibited in print ads or brochures may be prohibited on blogs as well, such as: (1) deceptive and misleading statements (such as guaranteed results) or statements that cannot be factually substantiated (e.g., "We are the best lawyers in town!"), (2) claims of specialization may also be prohibited, or (3) use of monikers or prohibited logos (such as "The Heavy Hitter" or a pit bull logo, which isn't allowed in Florida (*see* Will Hornsby, "Florida Court Takes a Bite Out of Advertising," **http://www .willhornsby.com/archives/news-florida-court-takes-a-bite-out-of- advertising.html** (Nov. 18, 2005)).

In contrast to print ads or brochures, blogs also present special ethics considerations. Because websites are viewable anywhere in the world rather than just a specific geographic location, they can give rise to potential claims of unauthorized practice of law (UPL). Accordingly, a blog that dispenses information on legal issues might need to specify the states where you are licensed to practice and can handle cases. Also in contrast to brochures, blogs may open the door for readers from anywhere to contact you by email, so be sure to include a disclaimer that sending an email does not trigger an attorney-client relationship, to prevent a reader from, for example, claiming that you never responded to her email and caused her to miss the statute of limitations on her suit.

If you publish an article in a journal or newspaper, you typically aren't required to include a disclaimer that your article is advertising. That's because many bars treat articles as educational tools rather than communications intended to attract paying clients. Under some bar rules, this same reasoning might apply to blogs which merely provide commentary or discuss case law rather than solicit business, thus exempting blogs from regulation as lawyer advertising. *See e.g.*, NY Rule 7.1 and comments (noting that blogs that serve a primarily informational function are not considered advertising). Again, check your bar rules because some specifically include blogs within the definition of "advertising" or define advertising in such a way that blogs fall within the scope of the definition.

So what types of issues do blogs raise? In addition to the considerations that apply to websites, one concern about blogs is that readers may rely on your advice and then try to hold you accountable if they relied to their detriment. You should consider including a disclaimer on your blog indicating that the posts address general matters and should not be relied on by readers or considered legal advice. Lawyers who blog should also avoid discussing "live" cases to avoid running afoul of court gag orders or inadvertently disclosing a strategy to opposing counsel. Finally, a recent law review article[1] suggests that blogging can raise ex parte concerns, though others disagree.[2]

Though not necessarily an ethics issue, for the sake of transparency, lawyers who blog disclose whether they have a personal interest in one side of an issue or not (for example, if you blog about a client that your firm represents, you ought to disclose that to readers). And if lawyers make recommendations about a product where they retain a financial interest (such as affiliate fees) or have an endorsement relationship with the company advertising the product, they should be wary of new Federal Trade Commission rules that crack down on undisclosed blogger endorsements (FTC, "FTC Publishes Final Guides Governing Endorsements, Testimonials," **http://www.ftc.gov/opa/2009/10/endortest.shtm** (Oct. 5, 2009)).

URLs
A website's URL or Web address can raise ethics issues in some jurisdictions. For example, some states prohibit use of phrases like "State X Law Clinic" or "Jones Legal Aid" because of the potential for confusion with bonafide legal aid organizations, and likewise prohibit use of these names for a website address (e.g., statexlawclinic.com). Don't assume that all states apply the same rules to law firm names and website URLs. In states like Texas (Rule 7.01), law firms are barred from using trade names (e.g., BlueSky Law Firm) but may use a trade name for a website or blog (e.g., **www.blueskylawfirm.com** as a website name so long as it is not deceptive). Likewise, North Carolina allows descriptive URLs, i.e. druginjury.com, as long as the website itself clearly identifies that it belongs to a lawyer or law firm (NC Bar, 2005 Ethics Opinion 14, **http://www.ncbar.com/ethics/ethics.asp?page=7&from=1/2006&to=6/2006** (Jan. 20, 2006)).

---

[1] **http://www.legalmarketingblawg.com/mt-static/html/lawreview.stanford.edu/content/vol61/issue6/RLee.pdf**
[2] *Drug and Device Law*, "On Ex Parte Blogging," **http://druganddevicelaw.blogspot.com/2009/05/on-ex-parte-blogging.html** (May 18, 2009).

Most state ethics codes offer fairly clear guidance on trade names and website names. Take the time to review them or you could potentially miss out on a desirable name because you mistakenly assumed that your ethics rules wouldn't allow it.

Rating Sites

As already mentioned, sites like Avvo rate clients. While lawyers won't be subject to an ethics complaint when a rating is performed by a third party, lawyers may be prohibited from using those ratings in ads and on websites in some jurisdictions.

The line of cases involving lawyer selection for *Superlawyers*, a publication that highlights lawyers selected by their peers as "super lawyers," offers some insight on how bars might resolve the issue of whether lawyers can link to third-party ratings sites like Avvo. In the *Superlawyers* cases, state disciplinary boards could not prohibit an independent publication from reporting on "super" lawyers. Lacking the ability to shut down *Superlawyers*, disciplinary boards turned their attention to regulating lawyers who featured their inclusion in *Superlawyers* on their websites. Initially, some jurisdictions chose to prohibit lawyers from publicizing their selection to the *Superlawyers*.[3] But most jurisdictions now give lawyers the leeway to advertise on these sites under certain conditions.[4] Generally, lawyers may not advertise their selection as a "Super Lawyer," but they may explain their selection for inclusion in a publication called *Superlawyers*. The Connecticut court gave the following example: "A Connecticut lawyer may not state that she has been selected as a super lawyer, but she may state that she has been designated a Connecticut Super Lawyer in *Connecticut Super Lawyers 2007* magazine."

If disciplinary boards apply the reasoning of *Superlawyers*, they would allow lawyers to list or link to an Avvo ranking on their website, perhaps with a caveat explaining that the ranking is performed by an independent provider and is not endorsed by the bar.

---

[3]The New Jersey Supreme Court's Committee on Attorney Advertising initially ruled (NJ Bar, Opinion 39, **http://www.judiciary.state.nj.us/notices/ethics/CAA_Opinion39.pdf**) that advertising on Superlawyers was unethical, but later amended NJ Ethics Rule 7.1(a)(3) to allow lawyers to link to a Superlawyers (or other) rating, with a disclaimer acknowledging that "No aspect of this advertisement has been approved by the Supreme Court of New Jersey."
[4]See Connecticut (**http://www.jud.ct.gov/SGC/Adv_opinions/Adv_07-00188.pdf**), Alaska (Alaska Bar, Ethics Opinion 2009-2, **https://www.alaskabar.org/servlet/content/2009_02.html** (Apr. 2, 2009)), and North Carolina (NC Bar, 2007 Ethics Opinion 14, **http://www.ncbar.com/ethics/ethics.asp?page=1&keywords=Super+Lawyers** (Jan, 25, 2008)) for such examples.

Testimonial Sites

Testimonials and endorsements are ethical red flags in advertising because they may create an expectation of success or discuss matters that cannot be factually verified (e.g., "My lawyer was the best!").

Websites like Avvo or LinkedIn allow clients and lawyers to post endorsements or testimonials, and where a third party outside the lawyer's control posts the testimonial (as opposed to the lawyer himself), it's doubtful that the bar would have the jurisdiction to require the third-party site to take down the post. At the same time, if a lawyer has control over testimonials at a third-party site, a bar could require a lawyer to monitor the postings and ensure compliance. Virginia Bar ethics counsel Jim McCauley opined that:

> Even if the state, like Virginia, allows client testimonials, endorsements, or recommendations, the testimonials must be monitored, revised, or removed so as to comply with Rules 7.1 and 7.2. For example, the lawyer cannot permit to remain on his LinkedIn page a client recommendation that says the lawyer is the "best personal injury lawyer in town," because it is a comparative statement that cannot be factually substantiated.[5]

The South Carolina Bar recently issued an opinion (SC Bar, Ethics Opinion 09-10, **http://www.scbar.org/member_resources/ethics_advisory_ opinions/&id=678**) warning that lawyers who have knowledge of a testimonial site and who link to it, or otherwise edit or solicit comments for it, must make sure that the listing conforms to ethics rules relating to solicitation and advertising. The opinion allowed that listings created, posted, and advertised by third parties would be outside the lawyer's control and therefore not subject to bar rules. The South Carolina opinion generated some difference of opinion[6] as to whether such limitations are constitutional and whether they are reasonable considering modern technology.

A separate ethics question arises where lawyers want to include a link on a website or blog to testimonials posted at a third-party site like Avvo. As

---

[5]Ethics Guru Blog, **http://ethicsguru.blogspot.com/2010/01/blogging-social-networking-for-lawyers.html** (January 19, 2010).
[6]*ABA Journal*, "Want to Update Your Avvo Listing? If So, Start Policing Client Comments, Opinion Says," **http://www.abajournal.com/news/article/want_to_update_your_avvo_listing_if_so_ start_policing_client_comments_opini/** (Oct. 28, 2009).

discussed earlier, a bar cannot prohibit clients from submitting testimonials to a third-party site; to do so is beyond the bar's jurisdiction and would violate clients' First Amendment rights. At the same time, some state discipline rules prohibit lawyers from posting testimonials on websites[7] or prohibit the inclusion of advertising.

The testimonials question, at least insofar as it relates to Avvo, is particularly complicated in Florida. In Florida, new advertising rules implemented January 1, 2010 (with a six-month moratorium on enforcement to allow lawyers to come into compliance) classify law firm websites, as well as other third-party sites like Facebook and Avvo, as advertising, and as such, are subject to the bar's advertising rules (with the exception of the prior-review requirements). Lawyers may include testimonials at their websites provided that the testimonials are shielded from view behind a disclaimer page, and accessed only when clients complete a form indicating that they understand the disclaimers. Florida Rule 4-7.2, as amended.[8] Would a website link to testimonials posted on a third-party site be subject to the same restrictions, i.e., would a lawyer have to accompany a link with the required disclaimer? That question remains unresolved as of the time this book went to press. But, given the broad scope of the Florida rules, many observers anticipate a constitutional challenge.

Endorsements
Lawyers who respond to colleagues' requests for endorsements may also run afoul of ethics rules prohibiting deceptive communications. For example, if a colleague who you know exclusively from social media sites seeks an endorsement but you've never met him, you should specify that in your testimonial (e.g., "I know John Smith from listserve X. Though we've never worked together, he has assisted me online with numerous questions regarding federal civil procedure. I also read his blog regularly and am impressed by the extent of his familiarity with this complex subject matter."). Be wary of reciprocal endorsements as well, which could be construed as a *quid pro quo* for a referral or recommendation, which many bars also prohibit.

---

[7] Arkansas (Rule 7.1(d), **http://www.law.cornell.edu/ethics/ar/code/AR_CODE.HTM#Rule_7.1**), Nevada (Rule 7.1(d), **http://www.leg.state.nv.us/courtrules/RPC.html**), among others.

[8] *See* B. Tannebaum, "My Law License" (December 24, 2009) at **http://ethicsguru.blogspot.com/2010/01/blogging-social-networking-for-lawyers.html** (describing new rule with citations).

Directory Sites

LinkedIn invites lawyers to list their "specialties," yet most bars do not permit lawyers to hold themselves out as experts. North Carolina practice management expert, Erik Mazzone, noted the potential ethics problem presented by LinkedIn, and advises lawyers to include a caveat in their entry, explaining that the practice areas listed are merely areas of focus and are not intended to suggest specialization, which the bar does not allow (or only allows certification). In Carolyn's view, this approach seems overly cautious: after all, it is unlikely that consumers will be duped into believing that a lawyer is a specialist based on a LinkedIn form that all participants, nonlawyers and lawyers alike, complete.

Social Networking Sites

Social networking sites like Facebook or MySpace allow users to upload photos and exchange personal information. Though there's certainly plenty of opportunity for stupidity in this regard (such as uploading photos of yourself drunk or wearing a skimpy swimsuit), stupidity alone won't necessarily trigger an ethics complaint. When it comes to social networking sites like Facebook, lawyers and even judges run into trouble when they attempt to use the site in a deceptive manner or engage in ex parte communications. Toward the end of 2009, a North Carolina judge was reprimanded for "friending" one of the lawyers in a case before him (*ABA Journal*, "Judge Reprimanded for Friending Lawyer and Googling Litigant," **http://www.abajournal.com/news/judge_ reprimanded_for_friending_lawyer_and_googling_litigant/** (Jun. 1, 2009)). Also in 2009, the Philadelphia Bar Association ruled that a lawyer could not ask a third party to "friend" a potential (unrepresented) witness in a case in order to gain access to the witness's *private* Facebook page (*Legal Ethics Forum*, "Legal Ethics and Facebook," **http://www.legalethicsforum.com/blog/2009/04/legal-ethics-and-facebook.html** (Apr. 29, 2009)).

Florida recently issued an opinion that judges should refrain from "friending" lawyers on Facebook.[9]

---

[9] FL. Supreme Court, Opinion No. 2009-20, **http://www.jud6.org/LegalCommunity/Legal Practice/opinions/jeacopinions/2009/2009-20.html**). *New York Times*, "For Judges on Facebook, Friendship Has Limits," **http://www.nytimes.com/2009/12/11/us/11judges.html?_r=1** (Dec. 11, 2009).

Twitter

At first blush, Twitter, a microblogging tool which allows users to exchange 140-character sound-bites, seems harmless enough. After all, how many ethics rules can you violate in just 140 characters?

Plenty, if you're not careful. A lawyer who tweets about a bad day in court ("Bad day. Case is a dud and we will lose.") may inadvertently convey client confidences or private deliberative work product to opposing counsel. Similarly, a lawyer who asks a follower who tweeted about a car accident whether she needs a lawyer may run afoul of bar rules prohibiting solicitation. Ethics rules don't prohibit lawyers from participating in Twitter, but neither does the limited scope of a tweet absolve lawyers from adhering to ethics requirements.

YouTube Videos

Most bars stringently regulate television advertising and thus, some lawyers have been transferring their video-based marketing to the Web through formats like YouTube. YouTube videos are far less costly than television ad campaigns, with circulation growing particularly in younger audiences. But YouTube is also appealing because some lawyers may believe that posting videos on YouTube shields them from bar regulation.

As with other types of online advertising, bar ethics rules apply to YouTube videos. Therefore, if you prepare a video with the sole intent of attracting clients—for example, one devoid of any substantive information, but simply screams "call 1-800-LAWYERS" or consists of a running series of client testimonials urging you to call the firm—chances are, it will be considered a form of advertising and subject to bar rules on disclaimers and prior review.

It is possible that YouTube videos may escape treatment as advertising, at least in some jurisdictions. In contrast to television advertising, many of today's lawyer-produced YouTube videos have a primary purpose of educating clients rather than soliciting them. Lawyers like New York Medical Malpractice lawyer Gerry Oginski often prepare a series of videos explaining how certain aspects of the legal process work. Whereas producing education-based video for television may not have been effective given the high cost of ads not to mention television audiences' short attention spans, the format works well for the Internet. Videos that simply convey information about a legal process, are really no different than newspaper columns or written materials except for format—and thus, in our view are exempt from state bar rules on advertising (nevertheless, you'll need to check the rules of your jurisdiction to determine whether and what forms of online videos are considered advertising). Florida and Texas have addressed this issue, holding that YouTube videos are subject to the ethics rules on lawyer advertising. Florida Rule 4-7.2 amended January 1, 2010; Texas Bar Website (**http://www.texasbar.com/ Template.cfm?Section=Advertising_Review**) (stating that YouTube videos are advertising and subject to prior review unless otherwise exempt).

CHAPTER SIXTEEN

The Legal Issues Related to Social Media

IN ADDITION TO GENERAL ethics rules, lawyers participating in social media should familiarize themselves with broader legal concepts relating to copyright infringement, FTC regulation, and defamation. Understanding broader legal issues is particularly important for lawyers who choose to outsource social media to virtual assistants or marketing companies so that they can ensure that their agents operate in a lawful manner.

Copyright

Many lawyers lack working familiarity with copyright law. Our advice: Gain a basic understanding both to protect your own work and avoid encroaching on others' copyright.

Protecting Your Own Work

Content is becoming an increasingly valuable currency in an online world where there's a 24/7 demand for fresh copy. As a result, it's possible that the content that you generate and disseminate through blogs, slide shows, or document archive sites could be harvested by others and republished for their own use. That's why it's imperative to protect your content with copyright.

Traditional Copyright

First of all, it is important to note that you don't have to do anything to create a copyright, other than commit a work with some originality to a fixed medium. Once your work is committed, a copyright exists that can protect your work for the duration of your lifetime and, depending on the jurisdiction, some period after your death. Registering a work will assist you in protecting or litigating your copyright, but it is not necessary in creating a copyright.

As part of copyright protections, you have the right to control any adaptations, distributions, or publications of your work. Copyright law, however, does not allow you to prevent any and all use of your work. The fair use doctrine allows some copying and distribution of your work without your permission. There is no exact definition for what comprises fair use, and the context in which the use exists, a classroom for example, might alter what fair use allows. Generally speaking, the amount of the work used and the market effect of the use will determine whether the unauthorized usage is acceptable. For general copyright information, Wikipedia is an excellent beginning source: **http://en.wikipedia.org/wiki/Copyright**.

Creative Commons Licenses

As noted above, authors do not typically need to register a work for copyright protections to take effect. What if an author does not wish to claim copyright protections? An author may choose to release a work under a Creative Commons License (CCL). (For general information, see Creative Commons, **http://creativecommons.org/**. For License text and description, see **http://creativecommons.org/about/licenses/**.) By using these licenses, an author may choose which copyright protections will apply. For example, an author may allow users to freely distribute a work as long as any subsequent distribution attributes the work to the original author. An author may even allow use of his work in derivative works (works based upon the original) but restrict what types of licenses the derivative author can use. There are several variations of these licenses. It is common to see material produced online distributed under a CCL agreement.

Protecting Your Copyrighted Material

It's one thing to be aware of your rights, but it's another issue to monitor others' usage of your online material and protect your copyrights. First of all, it is very easy for others to gain access to your copyrighted material. Whether they copy and paste the material directly from your site, either by navigating to your actual website or by using a RSS newsreader program, or use a computer program to remotely copy the material (typically referred to as screen scraping), once your material is published it is almost impossible to prevent a user from copying it in some form if they wish to do so.

One method for protecting your copyright is to clearly and prominently label your material as copyrighted material and explain what that entails for secondary users. Another method of protection is to digitally format your material. Instead of releasing material as text, you could publish it as a Flash file (a popular format that can work with graphics and text) or publish the material as a PDF document with built-in protections such as watermarking. A more expensive and comprehensive method is to employ copyright monitoring services. These services will actively monitor your copyrighted material, searching for unauthorized usage across the Internet. But, you can also create a free copyright monitoring service by using Google Alerts (or a similar product from any number of other search engines). With a Google Alert, anytime a search phrase you construct is found on a Web page Google searches, you will receive an email linking you to the website. Although not very useful for generic phrases, if you can construct a search based on a unique phrase in your material, this method might help in pinpointing usage that exceeds fair use.

Respecting Others' Copyright

Just as you'd like to preserve your own copyright, it's important that you avoid encroaching on others. Copyright law doesn't prohibit you from linking to other sites without permission so feel free to pass on links in blog posts, on Twitter, or at your online listing. But, copyright prohibits use of protected content or images without permission, except where terms of the copyright or license allow otherwise, or where you are merely making fair use of materials. So, consider the following rules of thumb.

Uploading or Archiving Documents

If you upload documents or video to an archiving site, be sure that you have rights to those materials. Because government-produced documents, such as reports, statutes, or case law aren't subject to copyright, you can upload those materials or post them on your blog without concern. Keep in mind that the terms of service with commercial research companies like LEXIS and Westlaw may prohibit you from redistributing cases. In addition, features like Headnotes are subject to copyright protection. So if you intend to post cases to a site, download the cases directly from the court website or from Google Scholar (which recently launched a free legal research service) to avoid any copyright or clickwrap restrictions.

Also, be wary when it comes to posting others' court filings. Even though most court pleadings and motions are part of the public record, that doesn't mean that they aren't subject to copyright law. After all, if someone photocopied James Joyce's *Ulysses* and filed it at the court, that wouldn't remove it from copyright protection. As a matter of fact, there are compelling arguments that briefs and pleadings are subject to copyright protection. *See* Volokh.com (July 23, 2009) (**http://volokh.com/posts/1248389303.shtml**) (explaining that the argument that briefs are protected by copyright is "moderately strong").

In fact, as the Volokh post notes, some lawyers have been asserting copyright violations against commercial research services for procuring and reselling their briefs online. To stay on the safe side, avoid mass uploads of others' work product to archiving sites unless you can justify it as fair use. For example, posting a copy of your opponent's brief that responds to yours at your blog is arguably fair use since it shows both sides of the argument. By contrast, posting every brief written by BigLawFirmX on your blog goes beyond fair use and would likely run afoul of copyright law. If you want to make available other lawyers' work product, link to it at their site and leave it at that.

Using Blog Posts

As we discussed earlier, linking to a blog post provides a great way to engage in conversation, and there's no need to obtain permission. Similarly, offering a snippet of a blog post to highlight your argument would fall within permissible fair use. However, a wholesale reprint of a blog post or news story, *even with a link and full attribution*, may implicate copyright concerns.

In addition, copying or republishing posts could yield a disciplinary proceeding. Grievance committees don't take kindly to plagiarism and there are several ethics rulings reprimanding lawyers for copying others' work.[1]

---

[1] Iowa attorney sanctioned for plagiarism, Order RE: Ruling on Motions for Sanctions, **http://207.41.19.195/decisions/20070821-pk-THEODORE_BLAIR_BURGHOFF.html** (Aug. 21, 2007); review of plagiarism sanctions in Minnesota, Martin A. Cole, "I Wrote This Article Myself," **http://www.courts.state.mn.us/lprb/93bbarts/bb0793.html** (1993).

Copyright Issues and Facebook and Twitter Posts

Can a user take a screenshot of your tweets or status updates on Facebook and republish it? Or would doing so infringe copyright? That's an issue that arose last year when a newspaper, without permission, published Dallas Mavericks owner Mark Cuban's stream of tweets criticizing the officiating at a game.[2] An issue of first impression, the matter of whether Twitter updates are protected by copyright has been the subject of much discussion around the blogosphere.

Some legal experts say that since most Tweets or status updates involve facts, they're not copyrightable, since copyright protects creative expression, not factual compilations. *See* Kyle-Beth Hilfer, *Tweet, Tweet Can I Copyright That*, Law Technology (January 19, 2010).[3] However, Hilfer concedes that there may be some "rare" Tweets that are succinctly original or creative to warrant copyright protection, in which case a court would need to examine whether republication constitutes fair use.

Photographs are another matter. Photographers generally hold a copyright interest in their photos, so taking photos from Facebook or off a user's social media profile and redistributing it without permission might raise copyright issues.

Many of the legal issues surrounding social media are new, and the law is still evolving. As social media gains traction, expect to see these issues emerge with more frequency.

Defamation

Defamation or libel (for written or otherwise published words) is the communication of a statement that makes a claim, expressly stated or implied to be factual, that may give an individual or company a negative image (**http://en.wikipedia.org/wiki/Defamation**).

Defamation cases have recently entered the new world of social media. Courtney Love was unable to get a case for defamation thrown out, even though the defamation supposedly occurred on Twitter (**http://www .contracostatimes.com/california/ci_13644062?nclick_check=1**). Lest you think that defamation by Twitter is merely for celebrities, a Chicago

---

[2]Consuelo Reinberg, "Are Tweets Copyright Protected," *WIPO Magazine* (July 2009), online at **http://www.wipo.int/wipo_magazine/en/2009/04/article_0005.html**
[3]**http://www.law.com/jsp/lawtechnologynews/PubArticleLTN.jsp?id=1202438916120&Tweet_Tweet_**

landlord sued a tenant for posting to Twitter allegedly defamatory statements regarding the condition of the apartment building (Chicago CBS 2, "Uptown Resident Sued for Twitter Post," **http://cbs2chicago.com/ local/twitter.post.lawsuit.2.1103625.html** (Jul. 27, 2009)).

It is not enough to only worry about your online activities if you run a social media site allowing users to post comments. In this case, your users' comments might be defamatory, but because they are anonymous or difficult to trace, a defamed individual or business might sue you as the forum provider. Luckily, Section 230 of the Communications Decency Act provides some protections for what it calls information content providers. Section 230 attempts to differentiate liability based on who is the actual speaker. A blog posting that induces defamatory comments should not open the blogger to liability. [See Electronic Frontier Foundation's Blogger's Section 230 FAQ, **http://www.eff.org/issues/ bloggers/legal/liability/230**.]

FTC Disclosure Issues

As mentioned earlier, ethics rules prevent lawyers from engaging in false or deceptive conduct while using social media. But in addition to professional rules, lawyers who blog must also abide by new FTC regulations that took effect at the end of 2009. The FTC Guidelines on Endorsements are meant to prevent consumers from being misled in cases where they might not realize that a blogger is receiving payment or some other benefit in exchange for a product endorsement.[4] Thus, FTC Guidelines advise companies and bloggers to disclose any endorsement relationships "clearly and conspicuously."

Occasionally, companies may send law bloggers free products (e.g., law practice management tools or books) to sample and review. Where a blogger receives the product for free, the FTC Guidelines require disclosure that the product reviewed is a gift.

---

[4]"FTC Publishes Final Guides Governing Endorsements, Testimonials," **http://www.ftc.gov/ opa/2009/10/endortest.shtm** (Oct. 5, 2009); Federal Register Notice, "Guides Concerning the Use of Endorsements and Testimonials in Advertising," **http://www.ftc.gov/os/2009/10/091005 endorsementguidesfnnotice.pdf**; Text of Revised Endorsement and Testimonial Guides, **http:// www.ftc.gov/os/2009/10/091005revisedendorsementguides.pdf**.

Final Words: Technology Is Here to Stay

Technology is here to stay and ignoring it no longer is an option. As we say in the title of the book, social media is the next frontier, but more accurately, it is just one component—albeit a critical one—of the 21st century law practice. Along with social media, a wide variety of technologies are changing our society and the legal profession as well. It's time for the legal profession to pull its collective head out of the sand when it comes to social media, emerging technologies, and the Internet.

Law firms and lawyers who turn a blind eye to technology do so to their own detriment, and their failure to acclimate to rapid technological change is going to catch up with them in 2010 and beyond.

Like it or not, technology has infiltrated nearly every aspect of life. All kinds of information, including the very latest news, is available online. Phone numbers, addresses, and contact information for every type of business is readily accessible on the Internet. Shopping can be accomplished quickly and securely with the click of a button. Music can be downloaded from iTunes. Movies and television shows can be instantaneously streamed through Netflix or Hulu.com directly to a high-definition television via a laptop.

Likewise, technology has infiltrated the legal profession and leveled the playing field in ways never before seen. Small offices now can compete on even footing with large law firms.

Entire offices can be operated remotely using reasonably priced Web-based tools and applications. Documents can be stored securely on remote servers. Law offices can use Web-based practice management and time and billing applications in lieu of the complicated and expensive software traditionally used by the legal profession.

Virtual law offices now are a reality and the value of online real estate has increased exponentially in recent years. With just a little effort, and minimal expense, solo practitioners can create a strong online presence that competes with that of larger firms.

The technologies are evolving at a rapid pace and changing the world around us on a global scale.

Lawyers Cannot Afford to Ignore Technology

Rest assured, our profession is not immune to the paradigm shift. Social media, cloud computing, mobile computing, realtime Web, and realtime search are some of the core areas predicted to be game changers over the coming year.

Lawyers cannot afford to ignore the trends and should, at the very least, make an effort to learn about them and understand the ramifications. It can never hurt to stay ahead of the curve, especially when most of your competitors don't even realize the curve exists.

The legal profession is just beginning to acknowledge the power of technology and the Internet. That's a start, but reluctant acceptance simply is not good enough.

We tend to carefully guard our profession and most lawyers are reluctant to make changes that might alter the way things have "always been done." We revere precedent and distrust change. As a result, we cling to the past, making decisions about technological change and innovation that ultimately harm our profession in the long run.

This is a mistake, since any lawyer who takes the time to research emerging technologies would wholeheartedly agree that these new platforms fundamentally change the practice of law. Lawyers who deny this fact are reacting emotionally, rather than intellectually.

These new technologies have the potential to radically alter the way in which legal services are delivered to consumers. Forward-thinking lawyers are embracing virtual law offices, cloud computing, social media, and collaboration tools. Innovative practitioners understand the importance of using emerging technologies in their law practice.

There has been much talk in recent years about pricing legal services differently, including the death of the billable hour and the increase of flat-fee services. However, the key to change is to deliver legal services effectively and efficiently. It ultimately boils down to delivering value to the legal consumer by working differently, rather than pricing the services differently.

The key to working differently is the utilization of emerging technologies. To do this, the legal profession as a whole must embrace technological change. Lawyers must make it a priority to learn about and understand new technologies and then incorporate them into their law practices.

Change Is Good

Law firms must change their culture. It's not simply a matter of utilizing one or two new technologies—it's a matter of changing attitudes. The youngest members of law firms are the key to accomplishing the attitudinal makeover that is required.

Generation Y lawyers are less attached to the status quo. These lawyers are part of the connected generation and grew up with the Internet. For them it's not business as usual; they understand how to use the new technologies and are not averse to change.

These lawyers are the future, and the inheritors, of the profession. Law firms should be generous benefactors and give their younger lawyers the opportunity to lead the charge to change. Because, as we all must understand—change is good.

The legal profession must learn to embrace, not fear, the changing landscape. There is still a demand for legal services, and there always will be—technology has not changed that fact. Technology has altered the playing field and the rules of the game by changing the ways in which legal services are marketed, sold, and purchased.

The change is not temporary, but permanent. Lawyers who accept and embrace that fact and position themselves for the future—rather than denying its reality—will prosper and profit in 2010 and beyond.

Will you be one of those lawyers?

Appendices

Appendix A

Ten-Step
Countdown to
Starting a Blog

INTERESTED IN GETTING A blog up and running? We could devote an entire book to legal blogging, but here are ten quick steps to getting started:

1. **Read.** Before you even start a blog, take a look around the blogosphere and get a sense of what other bloggers are doing. Reading blogs will give you a sense of what you like and don't like and will also help you figure out whether a particular topic is already saturated. For a full list of legal blogs divided by topic, visit the *ABA Journal* site at **http://www.abajournal.com/blawgs/by_topic/**.

2. **Settle on a topic.** Next, settle on a topic. With blogs, you're best off keeping the scope narrow since most visitors will come to the blog seeking specific information. If readers have to hunt through a cornucopia of posts to find the kernels that interest them most, they're not likely to return. If your practice encompasses several specialties, such as estates, criminal, and family law, you're better off starting a couple of blogs than trying to cover all these topics under one roof. A second reason for keeping a blog's scope narrow is to ensure that upkeep is manageable. If you choose a topic as broad as "criminal law" or "California law," you'll find yourself racing to cover multiple emerging developments.

3. **Settle on your intended audience.** Once you've come up with a topic, identify the target audience for your blog because that will inform the tone and subject of your blog posts. If you

blog for consumer clients, you'll want to explain basic concepts, address FAQs, (frequently asked questions) and discuss legal cases in a conversational tone geared for lay people. Alternatively, if your blog is intended to generate referrals from other lawyers, you can write about slightly more complex matters and also address topics in a way to showcase your analytical skills and familiarity with the topic.

4. **Pick a name.** What's in a name? Everything, when it comes to a blog. The name you select for your blog will drive traffic because each time you update the blog, Google will index it just a bit higher in the rankings. Your blog's title should always reflect the subject matter of the blog. Also keep in mind that geographic-based names (e.g., PeoriaIllinoisFamilyLawyer) make sense because they help you gain presence in local markets.

   Got a cutesy name for a blog that you can't resist which doesn't directly convey the subject matter? Invest in two names—your preferred name and a more sensible one, and redirect the names so they point at the same site.

   (What does redirect mean? When you register the name for your blog at a domain registration site (e.g., GoDaddy.com, Register.com), you can activate the settings so that when users type in the name you registered (e.g., **www.bigblueblawg.com**), they'll be directed to your blog site, which might have a domain name like **www.blogger.com/bigblueblawg.com**.)

5. **Choose a blog platform.** You have plenty of options for blog platforms, from fee services like Lexblog, Justia, and G2Media that serve lawyers, to low-cost services like Typepad and freebies like Blogger and Wordpress.com. On top of that, you also have the option of installing a blog yourself on server space and using templates like Thesis or Headway to develop it. How to pick? First, if you're not sure that you'll stick to blogging, begin on one of the free or cheap platforms to get started. If you're still going strong after a few months, you can upgrade to a costlier and more professional service.

6. **Commit to updates at least one to three times a week for three to six months.** The most important rule for a successful blog is to write early and often. By often, we mean one to three times a week for at least the first three to six months. Once you've gained a following and built up content, you can cut down on the

frequency. If you don't think you can manage to meet this post-ing goal, stockpile standard posts on general topics in advance to fill in the gaps. As for blogging early, putting up posts early in the morning when folks hit their news aggregators and Twitters will increase your traffic.

7. **Monitor traffic.** Most blogs offer some kind of stats package so that you can track the source of your traffic and learn what keyword searches bring visitors to the site. You can also install Google Analytics (**www.google.com/analytics**) at no charge. Understanding your traffic is important because it enables you to customize future posts to meet the needs of your audience.

8. **Join the conversation.** Once you start blogging, you can start engaging other bloggers. Comment at their sites, link generously to other bloggers' posts (but don't lift content without attribu-tion) and create some interaction.

9. **Don't focus on links and reciprocal links.** So many new bloggers obsess over getting links to their site. Relax. An outgoing link from another blogger won't yield much traffic. What's far more valuable are organic links—hypertext links that are embed-ded in the text of a post rather than links listed in the sidebar, or included as the result of a reciprocal arrangement. Organic links place higher in the search engines. Plus, readers are more likely to actually click through on the link to visit your blog where another blogger or website actually discusses it in a post and links to your blog by name. That kind of visibility is far more valuable than scoring a link along with dozens of others in someone's blog sidebar.

10. **Redistribute your content.** As we discussed in the text, there are many social media tools available through which you can redistribute blog content—RSS feed, Twitter, Facebook or LinkedIn, to name a few. You can also convert blog posts into longer articles that you can upload on sites like JDSupra.com or Scribd.com. Take advantage of these tools to disseminate your blog content widely.

Appendix B

A Mini Twitter Glossary

TWITTER HAS A VOCABULARY of its very own. Though you'll catch on soon enough by playing around on it, here's a quickie guide.

Profile: Basic information that you list about yourself on Twitter. At a minimum, your Twitter profile should include your photo, name, website, and email so that folks can contact you offlist. In Part III, we'll explain how to set up a profile.

Tweet: a 140-character communication. Throughout this book, you'll see several threads of tweets as examples. As you can see, it's possible to engage in a reasonably substantive, albeit terse, conversation even within the 140-character parameters.

Friends: Friends are the folks on Twitter whom you choose to follow.

Followers: Followers are those who sign up to receive your tweets.

Following: Following someone on Twitter means you will see their tweets in your personal timeline.

@: The @ sign denotes a user address on Twitter. When you send a message to a user with the @ sign, or post a tweet with their name preceded by the @ sign, they'll receive notice of it, and your followers will view it publicly as well.

Examples of @ sign use:

reading @lisasolomon's piece on smallLaw & outsourcing –
http://bit.ly/4r1a64 If you're a solo, have you outsourced to
foreign country?
7:15 PM Jan 12th from TweetDeck

> @nikiblack shares some behind the scenes collab lessons
> from our upcoming SocMed book http://bit.ly/5oKdtN
> 5:48 AM Jan 13th from TweetDeck

DM: Direct message, a feature that lets you contact a follower privately. If someone isn't following you, you can't use the DM feature (you can check their profile for their email and contact them offlist). To manually send a DM, type "d username" and then your message. The screenshot below shows how you'd send a direct message.

Screenshot showing DM feature.

RT: Retweet. If you receive a tweet that you like or that includes information that you want to pass on to followers, use the RT function (or the letters RT before the message). The RT function will let the original distributor know that her message was passed along and will distribute the information to your followers.

This is a screenshot showing a profile where the user has just used the RT function.

You can also "retweet" a message if you're using Twitter on the Web. If you run your mouse over the message, a "reply" and "retweet" option will appear (*see* screenshot below). By choosing "RT," your message will automatically be retweeted to your followers.

This screenshot shows the "Retweet" option on the Twitter webpage, which appears when you mouse over a message.

#: The hashtag signal creates a topical category that can be easily searched. Hashtags are frequently created for events tweeted by users so that other attendees and observers can easily follow the activity.

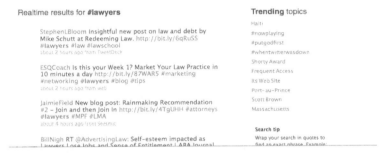

This screenshot shows a hashtag for lawyers. If you wanted to tweet about lawyers and have your tweet added to these results, you'd include #lawyers somewhere in your tweet.

Appendix C

Social Media Affinity Exercise

THIS CHART WILL HELP you identify certain goals of social media and get a sense of which systems might work for you.

Client Effective: Identify whether a particular social media system is effective for attracting a target client, with 1 being least likely to attract and 5 most likely.

Referral Effective: Identify whether a social media tool is effective for attracting referrals from other lawyers, with 1 being least likely and 5 most likely.

Affinity Scale: Rank whether you feel comfortable with this particular social media tool, with 1 being uncomfortable and 5 being desireable.

Cost: How much will the tool cost to implement? Rank your potential costs, with 1 being very expensive to 5 being free or low cost. In figuring out your costs, take into account factors such as whether you'll need to invest in a high-quality blog or support staff to implement social media.

Time Investment: Time investment is another factor. Will the tool require little time or substantial time to achieve your goals? Use 1 if you expect to spend more than 10 hours a week on social media through 5, if you anticipate spending three hours a week or less.

Scoring: Review your scores and select the top 2–3 tools with the highest scores. If all your high-scoring tools fall into the same category, consider diversifying—and adopting a lower-scoring tool from a different category.

Method	Client Effective (1–5 scale)	Referral Effective (1–5 scale)	Affinity (1–5 scale)	Cost (1–5 scale)	Time Investment (1–5 scale)	TOTAL
ONLINE						
Communications						
Blogs						
Twitter						
Community						
Martindale-Connected						
Facebook						
Lawyer Connection						
Legal OnRamp						
ABA (Legally Minded)						
Directories						
Avvo						
Justia/LII						
LinkedIn						
Justia						
Doc Archives						
JD Supra						
Docstoc						
Scribd						
YouTube						
SlideShare						

Appendix D

Recommended Reading

Anderson, Chris, *Free: How Today's Smartest Business Profit by Giving Something for Nothing.* New York: Hyperion, 2009.

Brogan, Chris and Smith, Julien, *Trust Agents: Using the Web to Build Influence, Improve Reputation, and Earn Trust.* New Jersey: John Wiley & Sons, Inc., 2009

Cashmore, Pete, Mashable Blog, **http://mashable.com**.

Friedman, Thomas, *The World is Flat: a Brief History of the Twenty-First Century.* New York: Farrar Straus and Giroux, 2006.

Godin, Seth, *Tribes: We Need You to Lead Us.* New York: Portfolio, 2008.

Qualman, Erik, Socialnomics-Social Media Blog, **http://socialnomics.net/**.

Vaynerchuk, Gary, *Crush It!: Why NOW Is the Time to Cash In on Your Passion.* New York: Harper Collins, 2009.

Appendix E

More Profile Creation Information

1. Setting Up a Facebook Fan Page

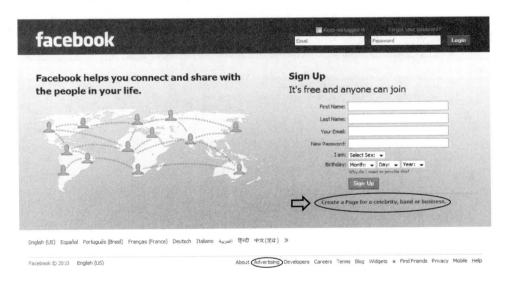

Step 1: How to access the sign-up link on the main Facebook page.

Step 2: Choose category and page name.

Step 3: Create your own profile.

Step 4: Privacy settings.

Step 5: Adding Twitter Stream.

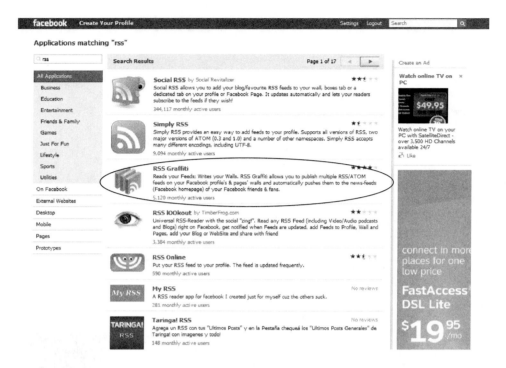

Step 6: RSS Graffiti—appears to be the only way to add Twitter stream to a Page—all the rest work for profiles, but not pages.

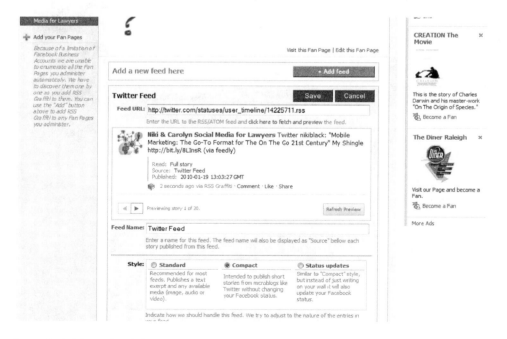

Step 7: Adding feed for Twitter stream to RSS Graffiti.

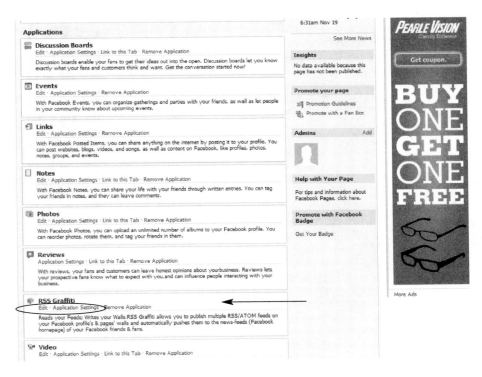

Step 8: Application now on Edit Page screen, can adjust settings such as tab or box displays.

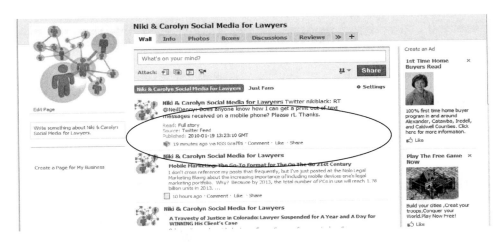

Step 9: Twitter feed now publishing to Wall.

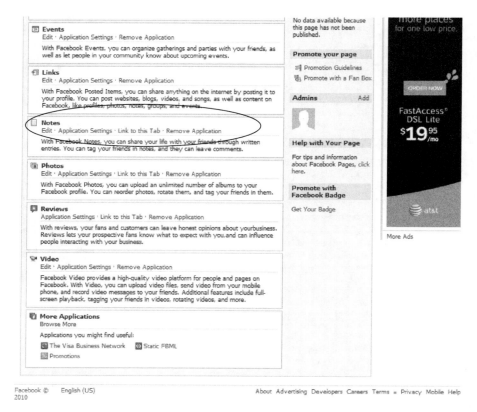

Step 10: Import Blog Posts—(Start by going to Notes section on Edit Page).

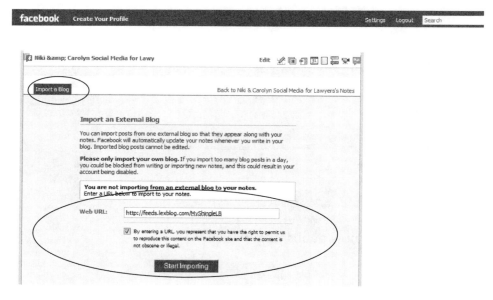

Step 11: Choose Import a Blog and add feed address.

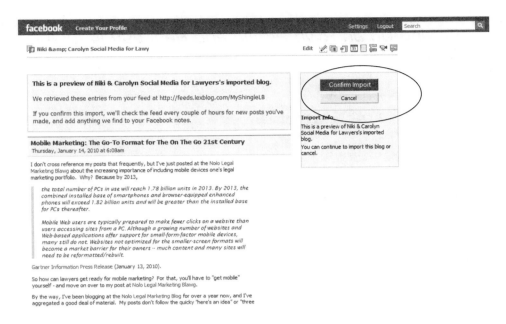

Step 12: Preview and confirm blog feed.

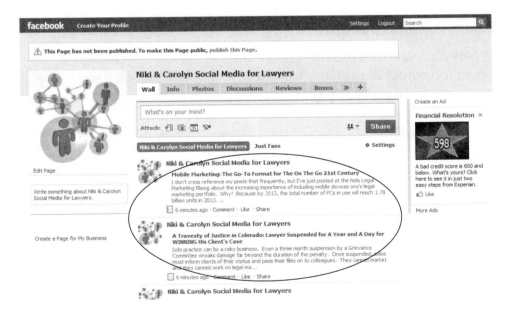

Step 13: Feed now appears on Wall.

2. Setting Up an Avvo Profile and Requesting Client Testimonial

Claim your Avvo Profile

When you visit the Avvo site, choose the "for lawyers" option in the upper top corner of the page. Choosing that option will take you to the above page where you can claim, i.e., set up your profile.

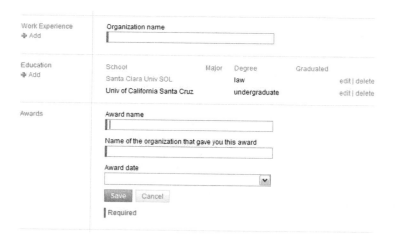

Once you've claimed your profile and registered, you can start completing the profile. Try to include as much information as possible since more robust profiles generally receive higher rankings. The process for completing the profile is similar to that for LinkedIn and Facebook, so we won't repeat it here.

After you've completed your profile, you can view it from the dashboard where it will look like this:

Underneath "Answers & Advice," you'll find the button where you can ask for client testimonials and endorsements:

When you select the option of seeking a client review, you'll see the following screen, which will allow you to send a request for a rating to clients. Be sure to include a personalized note in your request.

Client Rating Request
Invite your clients to rate you on Avvo.

From:

> smith@legalfirm.com

To (50 clients max):

> Enter up to 50 e-mail addresses
> e.g., joe@somedomain.com, jane@somedomain.com

Subject

> Jennifer Smith requests you submit a Client Rating on Avvo

Personal message   (3649 characters remaining)

> I've joined Avvo, a website that helps people find and choose lawyers. Avvo gives lawyers an online profile with space for ratings from former clients. If you feel comfortable recommending my services, I would welcome your comments for my Avvo profile. It only takes a couple of minutes and you can remain anonymous if you prefer.
>
> Thank you,
> Jennifer

Note: This is the message we'll send to your contacts along with instructions about how to rate you. Feel free to edit the note.

[Send E-mail] [Cancel]

Alternatively, you can also send a request for a rating to clients by email and include the following link directing clients to the ratings portion of the Avvo site: **http://www.avvo.com/review-your-lawyer**.

Index

Selected Books from . . .
THE ABA LAW PRACTICE MANAGEMENT SECTION

The Lawyer's Guide to Collaboration Tools and Technologies: Smart Ways to Work Together
By Dennis Kennedy and Tom Mighell
This first-of-its-kind guide for the legal profession shows you how to use standard technology you already have and the latest "Web 2.0" resources and other tech tools, like Google Docs, Microsoft Office and Share-Point, and Adobe Acrobat, to work more effectively on projects with colleagues, clients, co-counsel and even opposing counsel. In *The Lawyer's Guide to Collaboration Tools and Technologies: Smart Ways to Work Together*, well-known legal technology authorities Dennis Kennedy and Tom Mighell provides a wealth of information useful to lawyers who are just beginning to try these tools, as well as tips and techniques for those lawyers with intermediate and advanced collaboration experience.

The Lawyer's Guide to Marketing on the Internet, Third Edition
By Gregory H. Siskind, Deborah McMurray, and Richard P. Klau
In today's competitive environment, it is critical to have a comprehensive online marketing strategy that uses all the tools possible to differentiate your firm and gain new clients. The Lawyer's Guide to Marketing on the Internet, in a completely updated and revised third edition, showcases practical online strategies and the latest innovations so that you can immediately participate in decisions about your firm's Web marketing effort. With advice that can be implemented by established and young practices alike, this comprehensive guide will be a crucial component to streamlining your marketing efforts.

The Lawyer's Guide to Adobe Acrobat, Third Edition
By David L. Masters
This book was written to help lawyers increase productivity, decrease costs, and improve client services by moving from paper-based files to digital records. This updated and revised edition focuses on the ways lawyers can benefit from using the most current software, Adobe® Acrobat 8, to create Portable Document Format (PDF) files.

PDF files are reliable, easy-to-use, electronic files for sharing, reviewing, filing, and archiving documents across diverse applications, business processes, and platforms. The format is so reliable that the federal courts' Case Management/Electronic Case Files (CM/ECF) program and state courts that use Lexis-Nexis File & Serve have settled on PDF as the standard.

You'll learn how to:

- Create PDF files from a number of programs, including Microsoft Office
- Use PDF files the smart way
- Markup text and add comments
- Digitally, and securely, sign documents
- Extract content from PDF files
- Create electronic briefs and forms

The Electronic Evidence and Discovery Handbook: Forms, Checklists, and Guidelines
By Sharon D. Nelson, Bruce A. Olson, and John W. Simek
The use of electronic evidence has increased dramatically over the past few years, but many lawyers still struggle with the complexities of electronic discovery. This substantial book provides lawyers with the templates they need to frame their discovery requests and provides helpful advice on what they can subpoena. In addition to the ready-made forms, the authors also supply explanations to bring you up to speed on the electronic discovery field. The accompanying CD-ROM features over 70 forms, including, Motions for Protective Orders, Preservation and Spoliation Documents, Motions to Compel, Electronic Evidence Protocol Agreements, Requests for Production, Internet Services Agreements, and more. Also included is a full electronic evidence case digest with over 300 cases detailed!

The 2010 Solo and Small Firm Legal Technology Guide
By Sharon D. Nelson, Esq., John W. Simek, and Michael C. Maschke
This annual guide is the only one of its kind written to help solo and small firm lawyers find the best technology for their dollar. You'll find the most current information and recommendations on computers, servers, networking equipment, legal software, printers, security products, smart phones, and anything else a law office might need. It's written in clear, easily understandable language to make implementation easier if you choose to do it yourself, or you can use it in conjunction with your IT consultant. Either way, you'll learn how to make technology work for you.

The Law Firm Associate's Guide to Personal Marketing and Selling Skills
By Catherine Alman MacDonagh and Beth Marie Cuzzone
This is the first volume in ABA's new groundbreaking Law Firm Associates Development Series, created to teach important skills that associates and other lawyers need to succeed at their firms, but that they may have not learned in law school. This volume focuses on personal marketing and sales skills. It covers creating a personal marketing plan, finding people within your target market, preparing for client meetings, "asking" for business, realizing marketing opportunities, keeping your clients, staying in touch with your network inside and outside the firm, and more. An accompanying trainer's manual illustrating how to best structure the sessions and use the book is available to firms to facilitate group training sessions.

Many law firms expect their new associates to hit the ground running when they are hired on. Although firms often take the time to bring these associates up to speed on client matters, they can be reluctant to invest the time needed to train them how to improve personal skills such as marketing. This book will serve as a brief, easy-to-digest primer for associates on how to develop and use marketing and selling techniques.

The Lawyer's Guide to Concordance
By Liz M. Weiman
In this age, when trial outcomes depend on the organization of electronic data discovery, *The Lawyer's Guide to Concordance* reveals how attorneys and staff can make Concordance the most powerful tool in their litigation arsenal. Using this easy-to-read hands-on reference guide, individuals who are new to Concordance can get up-to-speed quickly, by following its step-by-step instructions, exercises, and time-saving shortcuts. For those already working with Concordance, this comprehensive resource provides methods, strategies, and technical information to further their knowledge and success using this robust program.

Inside The Lawyer's Guide to Concordance readers will also find:

- Techniques to effectively search database records, create tags for the results, customize printed reports, redline and redact images, create production sets
- Strategies to create and work with transcript, e-document, and e-mail databases, load files from vendors, manage images, troubleshoot, and more
- Real-world case studies from law firms in the United States and England describing Concordance features that have improved case management

The Lawyer's Guide to CT Summation iBlaze, Second Edition
By Tom O'Connor
CT Summation iBlaze gives you complete control over litigation evidence by bringing all you need—transcripts, documents, issues, and events, to your fingertips in one easy-to-use software program. Working in close collaboration with CT Summation, author and noted technology speaker Tom O'Connor has developed this easy-to-understand guide designed to quickly get you up and running on CT Summation software. Fully up-to-date, covering the latest version of iBlaze, the book features step-by-step instructions on the functions of iBlaze and how to get the most from this powerful, yet easy-to-use program.

The Lawyer's Guide to Microsoft Word 2007
By Ben M. Schorr
Microsoft Word is one of the most used applications in the Microsoft Office suite—there are few applications more fundamental than putting words on paper. Most lawyers use Word and few of them get everything they can from it. Because the documents you create are complex and important—your law practice depends, to some degree, upon the quality of the documents you produce and the efficiency with which you can produce them. Focusing on the tools and features that are essential for lawyers in their everyday practice, *The Lawyer's Guide to Microsoft Word* explains in detail the key components to help make you more effective, more efficient and more successful.

The Lawyer's Guide to Microsoft Excel 2007
By John C. Tredennick
Did you know Excel can help you analyze and present your cases more effectively or help you better understand and manage complex business transactions? Designed as a hands-on manual for beginners as well as longtime spreadsheet users, you'll learn how to build spreadsheets from scratch, use them to analyze issues, and to create graphics presentation. Key lessons include:

- Spreadsheets 101: How to get started for beginners
- Advanced Spreadsheets: How to use formulas to calculate values for settlement offers, and damages, business deals
- Simple Graphics and Charts: How to make sophisticated charts for the court or to impress your clients
- Sorting and filtering data and more

Find Info Like a Pro, Volume 1: Mining the Internet's Publicly Available Resources for Investigative Research
By Carole A. Levitt and Mark E. Rosch
This complete hands-on guide shares the secrets, shortcuts, and realities of conducting investigative and background research using the sources of publicly available information available on the Internet. Written for legal professionals, this comprehensive desk book lists, categorizes, and describes hundreds of free and fee-based Internet sites. The resources and techniques in this book are useful for investigations; depositions; locating missing witnesses, clients, or heirs; and trial preparation, among other research challenges facing legal professionals. In addition, a CD-ROM is included, which features clickable links to all of the sites contained in the book.

The Lawyer's Guide to Microsoft Outlook 2007
By Ben M. Schorr
Outlook is the most used application in Microsoft Office, but are you using it to your greatest advantage? *The Lawyer's Guide to Microsoft Outlook 2007* is the only guide written specifically for lawyers to help you be more productive, more efficient and more successful. More than just email, Outlook is also a powerful task, contact, and scheduling manager that will improve your practice. From helping you log and track phone calls, meetings, and correspondence to archiving closed case material in one easy-to-store location, this book unlocks the secrets of "underappreciated" features that you will use every day. Written in plain language by a twenty-year veteran of law office technology and ABA member, you'll find:

- Tips and tricks to effectively transfer information between all components of the software
- The eight new features in Outlook 2007 that lawyers will love
- A tour of major product features and how lawyers can best use them
- Mistakes lawyers should avoid when using Outlook
- What to do when you're away from the office

30-Day Risk-Free Order Form
Call Today! 1-800-285-2221
Monday–Friday, 7:30 AM – 5:30 PM, Central Time

Qty	Title	LPM Price	Regular Price	Total
_____	The Lawyer's Guide to Collaboration Tools and Technologies: Smart Ways to Work Together (5110589)	$59.95	$ 89.95	$_____
_____	The Lawyer's Guide to Marketing on the Internet, Third Edition (5110585)	74.95	84.95	$_____
_____	The Lawyer's Guide to Adobe Acrobat, Third Edition (5110588)	49.95	79.95	$_____
_____	The Electronic Evidence and Discovery Handbook: Forms, Checklists, and Guidelines (5110569)	99.95	129.95	$_____
_____	The 2010 Solo and Small Firm Legal Technology Guide (5110701)	54.95	89.95	$_____
_____	The Law Firm Associate's Guide to Personal Marketing and Selling Skills (5110582)	39.95	49.95	$_____
_____	Trainer's Manual for the Law Firm Associate's Guide to Personal Marketing and Selling Skills (5110581)	49.95	59.95	$_____
_____	The Lawyer's Guide to Concordance (5110666)	49.95	69.95	$_____
_____	The Lawyer's Guide to CT Summation iBlaze, Second Edition (5110698)	49.95	69.95	$_____
_____	The Lawyer's Guide to Microsoft Word 2007 (5110697)	49.95	69.95	$_____
_____	The Lawyer's Guide to Microsoft Excel 2007 (5110665)	49.95	69.95	$_____
_____	Find Info Like a Pro, Volume 1: Mining the Internet's Publicly Available Resources for Investigative Research (5110708)	47.95	79.95	$_____
_____	The Lawyer's Guide to Microsoft Outlook 2007 (5110661)	49.99	69.99	$_____

*Postage and Handling	
$10.00 to $49.99	$5.95
$50.00 to $99.99	$7.95
$100.00 to $199.99	$9.95
$200.00+	$12.95

**Tax	
DC residents add 5.75%	
IL residents add 10.25%	

*Postage and Handling	$_____
**Tax	$_____
TOTAL	$_____

PAYMENT

❏ Check enclosed (to the ABA)

❏ Visa   ❏ MasterCard   ❏ American Express

_____
Account Number   Exp. Date   Signature

Name _____ Firm _____

Address _____

City _____ State _____ Zip _____

Phone Number _____ E-Mail Address _____

Guarantee
If—for any reason—you are not satisfied with your purchase, you may
return it within 30 days of receipt for a complete refund of the price of the
book(s). No questions asked!

Mail: ABA Publication Orders, P.O. Box 10892, Chicago, Illinois 60610-0892
♦ **Phone: 1-800-285-2221** ♦ **FAX: 312-988-5568**

E-Mail: abasvcctr@abanet.org ♦ **Internet: http://www.lawpractice.org/catalog**